So Far, So Good

An Historian's Memoirs

So Far, So Good

An Historian's Memoirs

James C. Davis

P. M. Gordon Associates, Inc.

PHILADELPHIA ❈ 2008

Library of Congress Control Number: 2008902867

ISBN: 978-0-9788636-2-3

To order single copies of this book,
please visit Amazon.com.

To place bulk orders or for information
about rights and permissions, email the author at
jamescdavis@verizon.net.

To my brother Bill

OTHER BOOKS BY JAMES C. DAVIS

The Human Story:
Our History, from the Stone Age to Today (2004)

Rise from Want:
A Peasant Family in the Machine Age (1986)

A Venetian Family and Its Fortune, 1500–1900:
The Donà and the Conservation of Their Wealth (1975)

Pursuit of Power:
Venetian Ambassadors' Reports on Spain, Turkey, and France
in the Age of Philip II, 1560–1600 (editor, translator, 1970)

The Decline of the Venetian Nobility as a Ruling Class (1962)

CONTENTS

To the Reader   ix

ONE   Joiner of Circles   *1*

TWO   Hunter of Truth   *19*

THREE   Cold Warrior   *37*

FOUR   On My Way   *57*

FIVE   Lives of Rich and Poor   *80*

SIX   Wordstruck Klutz   *99*

SEVEN   A Global View   *119*

EPILOGUE What Next?   *138*

Notes   *139*

Index   *143*

TO THE READER

THESE MEMOIRS ARE about me of course but also about the world in which we live, both you and I.

This is who I am. I grew up with "advantages"—not money, just advantages—and to these I added great good luck. For more than fifty years I've been an historian, that is, an explorer searching backward, learning how we humans used to live.

The book should interest those who want to know how a child's awareness of the world expands, how young people look for answers, how Americans perceived the Cold War, how historians go about their work, and whether life on Earth is getting worse or better.

I'm grateful to my wife Elda who, when I threw out a box of my old letters, rescued and saved them until I needed them when I wrote this book. (Fifty of them are now in the General Manuscript Collection of Princeton's Mudd Library.) For several kinds of help I also thank my friend and former colleague Bruce Kuklick, my brother Bill, and dependable Mia Macintosh.

Joiner of Circles

WHEN WE'RE CHILDREN we glide, scarcely knowing it, from awareness of a tiny circle of Giant People around us, to awareness of a larger ring, and then a larger one, and on and on.

Of course I don't recall this, but probably I started to be aware that my parents were separate people, with minds and feelings of their own, when I was two and a half or three years old. That's when children usually make that change.[1]

After I had crossed that line and reached awareness of the separateness of others I adored our mother, as did my older brothers, whom you'll meet below. Mary Davis was born in an iron town near Philadelphia where her father was cashier of a company that made enormous wrought iron bridges. In an age when few young women went to college, she and her two sisters went to Sweet Briar in Virginia, where, because their last name (then) was Pennypacker, their classmates knew all three as "Penny." She was pretty, and she told us that once, in Philadelphia, she had chanced to meet the famous conductor Leopold Stokowski, who later had a well-known love affair with movie actress Greta Garbo, and he chatted her up. She married my father in 1924.

She kept a baby book for my brother Bill, her first-born child. In addition to recording his pounds and ounces and other weighty matters she would add remarks, such as "Bill is absolutely fearless with dogs" or "Bill [in the bathtub] shows natural swimming ability." Later, for my brother Dick, her second child, she penned some information about him into Bill's baby book. I, the third and last, never rated any mention in this book.

Even so, people used to say, and one of my aunts positively delighted in telling me, that when I was a child my mother spoiled me. According to this unlikely tale, because she had two older boys and much to do, she found it easiest to let me do as I pleased.

My father, Faber Davis, was born in New York City not merely in his grandparents' brick-and-brownstone house but in the same room and most likely the same bed in which his mother had been born. But he grew up in a New Jersey town that I'll describe below. It's said that once he threw some water on his sister from a second floor balcony but fell and broke his arm, having neglected to let go of the bucket.

His father died when he was young, and he was something of a handful for his widowed mother. So, fatefully for him, she sent him to a summer camp for boys, Awosting, which stood on cliffs above a mountain lake in New York State. In 1912 he graduated from Princeton. I recently discovered in his class's graduation yearbook that 25 of his classmates claimed (in response to a questionnaire) that they chewed tobacco, and half reported that they'd kissed at least one girl. During World War I my father drove an ambulance in France.

The camp he went to as a boy, however, was the big thing in his life. He went there as a "camper" and then as counselor every summer (except when in the Army), and eventually he owned and ran the camp.

He was 42 when I was born, and that fair-sized age gap sometimes made it harder to feel close to him than to my mother (who was younger). However, our disparity in age was nothing like the one between my great-great-great-great-great-grandfather Gabriel Leggett and his last two children, who were twins. They were born in the late 1770s after Gabriel married for the third time when he was over 80. Now *that's* a gap.

In any case, my father was a kindly man and first-rate teacher. He could explain to a frightened little boy what thunder is or, later, what the "fourth dimension" is. (He said some thought it might be time.) Once he even explained to me why advertising serves a purpose. (It lubricates the wheels of trade.)

In addition to my parents, I had the brothers who got attention in the baby book. Bill was (and is) five years older than I, and knew all there was to know. Dick (who died in 2007) was three years older, and easy to get along with. If he didn't want to do something, he'd say, "Let's not, and say we did." We had a dog named Bingo, who looked like a small, white, smiling pig. If you didn't watch her, when her bath was finished she would slip outside and roll in what the milkman's horse had dropped beside the curb.

GRADUALLY I LEARNED my way around. The second, larger circle I moved into was our street.

The house where I was raised was right beside the house in which my father had been raised, halfway up Fairview Avenue. Fairview didn't offer any view to speak of, fair or foul, but it was steep and good for sledding, which was greatly in its favor. When it snowed a family at the bottom of Fairview used to scatter ashes from their coal furnace on the street to prevent our sledding into traffic.

As a little boy I found our Fairview neighbors hard to figure out. In the house across the street lived the widow of a broker. The way I understood it, he had jumped from a high window when the stock market crashed in 1929, but I later learned that he had died of natural causes. In the house below the widow

With my Flexible Flyer

lived, or so I thought, the well-known opera singer, Lily Pons. In fact this person was a young woman named Lilly who had an office job and walked with a limp caused by childhood polio.

I was certain that a robber lived inside the abandoned house two doors up the hill from ours because I saw him once when coming home from school. He was in a second-story window staring down at me, and I knew he was a robber because he wore a black cloth mask.

On the lower side of our home was the house my father had grown up in. His sister's family lived there, and my cousin Jack was my best friend. Farther down the hill lived a Lutheran minister and his family. For some reason his wife wanted us to call her older son Bob, not "Fat." Fat Freitag.

I DIDN'T TAKE THIS IN at first, but we who lived on Fairview helped to fill a narrow zone between two neighborhoods, one rich, one poor.

As my view enlarged and I stepped inside this larger circle, I began to notice the imposing houses in the blocks beyond the upper end of Fairview. It wasn't hard to understand, even in those pinched Depression years, that those who lived up there were thriving, even rich. One family owned a lot of land and an apple tree some of whose fruit Jack and I once stole. At Halloween we'd ring the doorbells of those grander homes, skipping Fairview on the theory that the wealthy give you more. A butler sometimes met us at the door, holding out a bowl of candy corn.

On the other hand, those who lived beyond the bottom of our street were fairly poor. We called this place "the Valley" and through it flowed a dirty stream we called "the Banana Peel." Many people in the Valley were "Italians," meaning Italian-Americans. These included a high school girl who often baby-sat my brothers and me in the afternoon, after she and we got out of school. As a little boy my brother Bill had named her "Dodo."

Once my father drove me to a second hand store to help me buy a cabinet for my rocks and minerals "museum." The owner was an "Italian" named Tulio, who enchanted my father (an opera lover) by telling him that he had seen the famous tenor Enrico Caruso sing a note at just the proper pitch and break a wine glass. (I've looked this up. It's hard to do, perhaps impossible.) Tulio had for sale a cabinet that was nearly perfect; its only defect was a missing door. When my father told him that "This boy doesn't have much money," I cried, "I have two *dollars*!" So we paid two dollars.

Also in the Valley was a factory where women painted numerals on watches, using paint that glowed in the dark because it contained radium. They pointed their brushes with their lips, and many later died of cancer.[2]

EVENTUALLY I CAME to understand that our neighborhood was part of a circle even bigger. We were in the town of Orange, which boasted of a love song: "When it's Apple-Blossom Time in Orange, New Jersey, We'll Make a Peach of a Pair." In time I learned that Orange, like its cousins, East, West, and South Orange (there isn't any North one), was a suburb of Newark, and, what was more important, of the great metropolis, New York.

You could reach New York, in whose shadow we were living, on a train line called the Delaware, Lackawanna, and Western, or DL&W. People said those letters stood for Delay, Linger, and Wait. But my father sometimes drove the family to New York, where we'd see such famous ocean liners as the *Normandy* and *Rex* moored beside the piers. New York City had museums with dinosaurs and suits of armor, and the Empire State Building, then the tallest structure in the world. Once my next-door uncle took my cousin Jack and me on an airplane flight from Newark to New York and back.

As I was orienting myself in family, neighborhood, and town, I was also doing so among the social classes. As a boy I asked my father once if we were poor. Did I ask him that because I knew about the poorer people in the "Valley"? I doubt that since, to me, being poor looked noble and romantic. I think I got that notion from a children's book, *Hans Brinker or the Silver Skates*. (Hans is a Dutch boy who's so poor that he races on skates with wooden blades. He and his sister want to win a skating prize to pay for an operation for their father, who was injured in a fall from a scaffold.) In any case my father humored me and said he did suppose that we were poor.

As a child in the 1930s, I was far too young to understand the pain that many suffered in those Great Depression years. I do recall an evening when my parents, my brothers, and I were eating in a cafeteria, and my father saw a man eating scraps that others had left on their plates. He gave this man some money, and we saw him buy a sandwich.

While others went without, we got by all right. My father had inherited a little money from his mother, and he also made a modest living from Awosting. However, my brother Bill informs me there were summers in the '30s when the camp lost money. Other "Depression babies" claim that growing up when times were hard had made them frugal, but that wasn't true for me.

My earliest recollection that I can date has to do with school, another of those circles I was stepping into. In the spring of my kindergarten year I asked our assistant teacher for several of the little pictures of rabbits that we stuck, like stamps, on drawings. She said she had no more to give me because those were Easter bunnies and Easter now had passed. So that must have happened just about the time that I turned six.

You might suppose that one who later on would teach would have liked to go to school. Not me. I like to say that I flunked kindergarten. Once we formed a circle and played a game based on the song "A Tisket, a Tasket, a Green and Yellow Basket." You may have played it too. One child ran around behind the others, dropped a little basket behind another child, and scampered back to his or her own place. But Jimmy didn't understand this complicated game and our grouchy teacher, Miss Haney, was quite unkind about the matter.

In a playlet we put on in second grade I played a giraffe. (This was clever casting; I was tall.) A classmate played some other beast, and at a certain point she didn't say her line, which was supposed to be my cue. So naturally I did not say my line. From the wings our teacher hissed at me, but of course I wouldn't say my line till Emily said hers. Miss McLaughlin drew the curtain, and was furious with me.

The children in our school included well-off ones from the streets above us, middle-income kids like me, and poor ones from the Valley. Once my fifth grade teacher urged a Valley boy to move a little faster, and he told her cheerfully to "Hold your water, sister!" I had never heard that pungent turn of phrase but our teacher had. She was stunned at first, then exploded.

When the children in my class at school lined up by height, I was always at the end along with George Prolesdorfer, another ectomorph. This was in the late 1930s and George's family had fled from Germany because of Hitler's persecution of his country's Jews.

Usually I was far too awed by teachers to get into trouble. But in my sixth grade year I somehow misbehaved one time, so the teacher ordered me to stay in school after all the other kids had left for home. Then she told me she was shocked by my behavior. She said that she had taught my older brothers, who were always little gentlemen.

To judge by my father's father's schooling, she could have been far harsher than she was. My grandfather, Henry Davis, once wrote a friend that in "old Ireland" the Reverend Joseph Cooper "caned me and the other boys in Latin with a rattan [wooden rod] on our hands and sitting downs until one day we had each received 32 times, then the clergyman came [to the Davis] home and told my father [that] he ought to kill me."

But going to school in America, two generations after my grandfather did in Ireland, was grim enough. Decades later, when my wife and I visited our children's school in the evening to meet their teachers, as soon as I saw the tiny desks and chairs and crayon drawings thumb-tacked on the walls I'd feel a wave of gloom.

RELIGION WAS MORE OR LESS like school, a circle to avoid. Here's another point I can illuminate with family history. In 1841 my great-grandfather Thomas William Monsell, another Anglo-Irish Protestant, wrote as follows from Dublin to his oldest child, my great-grandmother.

> My dear and dearest Mary Anne,
>
> I was extremely gratified to hear [that] you, P [Peter] & Bess had good marks at the Sunday School. That is the real joy to me. Oh how sweet the [?] to hear that my three darling little chicks have a love to [?} about God, feel a pleasure in thinking and talking about dear dear Jesus, who is ever a friend to little children . . . [He continues in this strain for a long paragraph.] Methinks I see you P and Bess up right early every morning to look over the [Bible] verse Mama explained the night before.

I'm glad he didn't have a chance to drench me in his cloying faith.

In 1801 my American great-great-grandmother, Mary Marsh, stitched a sampler with a prayer that ended with these priggish lines:

> But grant me that blest frame of mind
> Where no vain thoughts intrude,
> That blest serenity which springs
> From conscious rectitude.

My parents didn't overdo religion even though at their summer camp my father ran the weekly Protestant service. For me that fact gave him a confusing aura, part religious, mostly not. Before we boys at camp would go to bed at night we all would kneel beside the campfire while a counselor read a prayer or two. These often included one I like, although I'm not a believer:

> Oh Lord, support us all the day long until the shadows lengthen, and the evening comes, and the busy world is hushed, and the fever of life is over. Then in thy mercy grant us a safe lodging, and a holy rest, and peace at the last.

Before the evening meal at home my father always said the shortest grace he knew: "*Benedictus benedicat,*" which means, "May the Blessed One bless." We were ordinary, middle-level Episcopalians, but once he took me to a service at a "high" Episcopal church in the "Valley." He may have had a secret love of incense and the way the "priest" (not "minister") would chant, not speak the prayers.

My mother was more religious than he was, possibly because she grew up in a very observant family. (I'm aware of that because I edited a portion of her brother's memoirs.[3]) On Sundays her father used to attend a communion service at 7:30 a.m., after which his children went to Sunday school, in which he taught. The whole family then attended the 10:30 a.m. service, and most of them also attended the 7:30 p.m. evening service. All this church-attending as a girl hadn't made my mother stickily devout.

Of course, my brothers and I went to Sunday school. In a Christmas pageant I once played one of the Three Kings, carrying my father's brass cigarette box which *sort of* looked like gold and *could* have held some frankincense and myrrh. In Sunday school we sang such hymns as "Onward Christian Soldiers," and while at camp in the summer we might sing Kipling's stirring hymn, "Recessional":

> Lord God of Hosts, be with us yet,
> Lest we forget—lest we forget.

and George Doane's

> Fling out the banner! Let it float
> Skyward and seaward, high and wide . . .

Although we did sing hymns we also sang the Bible-spoofing "Sunday School Song," which holds that

Adam was a gardener and Eve a gardeneress.
They raised Cain and Abel, and sauerkraut and cress.
Eve ate an apple in the garden by the well
And now we know a tummy ache's the worst kind of . . .
[GIGGLES].

It's difficult to mention even the moderate tone of our religiosity without suggesting that religion mattered a lot to us. I believe it didn't. Well not to me at any rate. As children mostly do, I accepted my parents' religion in a casual way. It was like a cap you don or doff without a thought.

WHEN IT CAME to teaching values, my father's camp, Awosting, was quite another thing from school and church. My brothers and I were lucky that our father ran a summer camp for boys, since he could only afford to let us go there because he ran it. My vibrant childhood recollections aren't about the 42 weeks a year I spent at home, but the ten I spent at camp. You lived more in a day at camp than in a month at home.

The camp was in Connecticut. I didn't know the "old camp" in New York, the Awosting that my father went to as a boy and later ran, but I heard a lot about it and several times I've seen the site. It offered many things, including danger. The lake was clear as glass and frighteningly deep. If you'd drowned and slowly settled on the bottom, how could anyone have got you up? Running through the cliffs around the lake were thin crevasses in the rock—the Lemon Squeezer and the Fat Man's Misery—that boys would inch through at the risk of getting stuck until they'd shrunk enough to slither out. Around the camp were woods where one could easily get lost. They were said to be full of loutish blueberry pickers from the slums of New York City, and convicts who had escaped from a nearby prison for the criminally insane.

But my father only rented all that land, and at the end of the summer of 1934 (when I was three) the landlord told him that his lease was at an end. Angrily my father wrecked the improvements he had made, whereupon the landlord sued him and won a small amount of money. My father moved the camp to Bantam Lake, Connecticut, and there he ran it for another dozen years.

The "new camp" is the one that I recall. I started "going to camp" at seven, and each summer after that I shared a cabin with the same small group of friends. I arranged that with my father—a benefit of being the owner's son. The 50-or-so boys in the camp mostly came from well-off suburbs of New York, and they included "Mousey," "Duke," "Biggy," "Buzz," "Zwiggy," "Zuzu," and "Paint," who was fresh as.

A boy at camp named Roger later changed his first name and won a global reputation as the violinist, Ruggiero Ricci. He went to camp before me, so I never knew him, but when we both were old I wrote him, asking if he still recalled the camp. He answered that indeed he did. Once, he wrote, he'd called my father "Davis," and my father had reproved him

Who noticed, much less cared, that the mess hall and the cabins where we slept were shabby, and the bark was peeling from their logs? They stood upon a hundred splendid acres, and I knew the most enthralling spots: A grove of birches where (I then believed) a tribe of Indians once had lived. A field of goldenrod and orange devil's paintbrush. A former apple orchard, full of twisted, falling trees. A tiny stream that crossed the sandy beach to reach the lake. A scary yet alluring swamp.

It was not our church and schools in Orange that imbued our values, not mine at any rate. It was Camp Awosting, with its stress on "character" and growth. Comic books were frowned on and we were urged to use our time as if we'd bought it at great price. I won a prize one year for "taking advantage of one's opportunities."

At camp you learned the things that everyone will need to know, such as how to tie the knots you use when loading ships, or how to start a fire with flint and steel. (That's good to know if you are lost and thought to bring along those things.) And you learned the value of neatness. A careful boy, and much aware of the burden of being the director's son, I was often cited after Saturday "inspections" for having the neatest trunk.

I was bad at most sports, worse at others. My father loved baseball even more than opera, and in the afternoons he used to stretch out on the grass behind first base, beneath a giant hickory tree, and watch the games. I must have been a disappointment to him. Once I was a victim of the "hidden ball trick": I somehow got to first, but the first baseman hid the ball behind his back and when I stepped off base he tagged me.

Every year I played right field, where I could do least harm. To pass the time there I would hunt for interesting rocks, but now and then a player hit a ball my way. My teammates all would shout, "Wake up!" and if I found the ball I'd lob it to my brother Dick, in center field, hoping he knew what to do.

My father's cousin, Stuart Faber, was head counselor, and he taught me tennis, which I loved. It was Stu who gave me my first racket, a used one. I liked it even though it bore a little picture of a woman player, Alice Marble.

In his other role, nature counselor, Stu taught my brother Dick and me to identify a host of trees and flowers. In this way we earned points for our club, the Iroquois. I only wish I knew a quarter of those names today. Once he took me birding in the early morning and in the woods we heard a hermit thrush, a bird that's hard to find and shy. Stu and other boys and I would sometimes take a boat and drag a sack along the surface of the lake to scoop up plankton Stu would feed to fish he kept in tanks.

In real life (fall to spring) Stu lived near us in New Jersey, and once he took some friends and me to see a quarry with some splendid rocks. Another time he had my mother drive me to the high school where he taught biology so that I could view amoebas through a microscope.

Going to camp was not always good times, not at all. (In fact, my cousins Jack and Ed both went there and they didn't like it.) I remember feeling blue about my hopelessness at sports, a matter more important then than now.

Ever since I went to camp I've had this fantasy: I'm back at camp. Once again I'm just an awkward boy but *now* I have an adult's savvy. Batter up! I step up to the plate. The pitcher is a boy who in another game had yelled at me, "What's the matta? Never seen a curve before?" Everyone is sure that I'll strike out. I scorn the first two pitches, but the third is *mine,* and as I swing I WATCH THE BALL (Rule 1) and FOLLOW THROUGH (Rule 2). Because the shortstop drops the ball, I safely get to first. And there, aiming to distract the pitcher, I make a show of brushing off some nonexistent dust. As another batter steps up to the plate I take two steps off base. (I'm slow; that's all I'd better risk.) I hold my arms out, wave them up and down. The pitcher turns to glance at me. I know I'm on his mind. . . .

In 1947 my father sold Awosting, and the new owner/director was arrested one year later for "public lewdness." He sold the camp to Ozzy Ebner, who had been a counselor when my father ran the camp, and to this day Ebner's sons and grandsons run the camp. It now is more than a century old, the "oldest private boys summer camp in continuous operation."

ALL THINGS OLD enthralled me. That's another way in which my vistas grew, from circle on to circle.

We sometimes drove from our suburban New Jersey home to my mother's mother's house in Pennsylvania. Five humans and a dog would squeeze inside our car, my father puffing on a cigarette. Little things might liven up the trip. One of us would spot some Burma Shave advertising signs, spaced 20 feet apart, and in chorus we would read them: "Don't hurry up / To save a minute. / You need your head! / Your brains are in it. / Burma Shave."

After we had crossed the Delaware River and entered Pennsylvania the old things that I came to love appeared. Now the houses had a used and mellow look, and on some corner in each town or village you would see an old hotel named "King of Prussia Tavern" or "The General Johnson Inn."

My grandmother's house in the small iron-making town of Phoenixville where my mother had grown up looked very old to me and so did she, though she was younger than my present age. In her house were portraits, silhouettes, tintypes, and faded sepia photographs of solemn bearded men and lace-capped women. I slowly came to understand that I was linked to them by blood. (Today we'd say "by genes.")

Only recently I worked this out: As a girl in that small town in the 1870s my grandmother almost surely knew a certain boy who went to her school and whose house was only several blocks from hers. At age 15 he left the town and went out west, where he made his living robbing banks. Out there they knew him as . . . the "*Sundance Kid.*"

At Camp Awosting, just as in eastern Pennsylvania, one might see ancient things. I searched for Indian spearheads in the birch grove in the center of the camp, and I found a number of them, some in places where I would have sworn I recently had searched. They were slim, and flaked from snow-white quartz. I always showed the ones I found to Stu Faber.

Once I searched for spearheads in a pebbly section of the lakeshore, a place where I had never looked before. And here, among a million little stones, I found a spearhead unlike any I had ever seen. Instead of being slim and white, this one had three equal sides and had been chipped from cocoa-colored stone.

Nothing in my life has ever thrilled me like the finding of that spearhead. Nothing. Not just the finding, but the sensing what (I thought) it meant. Clearly this was made by other Indians, intruders on the lake, maybe enemies, different from the locals who had chipped those slender spearheads out of milk-white quartz. In my hand I held the evidence of long-past Indians unlike those I thought I knew.

About three decades later I visited Stu Faber in New Jersey. He was now an old, old man, and what he said surprised me. Even now I'm laughing at myself. The spearheads, not the brown one but the white ones made of quartz, had of course been planted in the center of the camp by Stu himself. He had found them somewhere else, and he left them where he knew we boys would find them. So the equal-sided cocoa-colored spearhead didn't come from elsewhere. On the contrary, it was probably the only one I found that local Indians had made.

Well never mind. Long before I learned the truth, the planted white ones and authentic brown one had, together, worked their magic on my mind.

VERY SLOWLY I began to learn about another circle, another zone of our existence, namely sex. Adults don't exactly hide the "facts of life," but neither do they shout them out. When I was very small I saw a headline in my parents' *New York Times* about arrests made in a "house of prostitution." When I asked my mother what that was, she said it was a place where naughty women lived.

When my parents took me to see "The Merry Widow" I was embarrassed by the cancan—dancing women showing us their silk-bedizened rears. My father noticed my reaction, and he later told me this was not considered naughty.

When I was maybe nine years old I asked a farmer about horses—how you told a female from a male. "By the ears," he said. My Hartwell cousin Bobby heard that fib and wised me up.

Children slowly figure out the "facts of life." I remember how a boy at Hill School (where I later went) slyly showed me (HUSH!) a photo of a naked girl.

MEANWHILE, IN THE larger world that I knew nothing of, other things were happening. For example, World War II.

This future historian of the world didn't know what lay beyond one smidgen of his country. It's true that I had read about that noble boy in Holland, Hans Brinker, and I'd heard my father's stories of "the War." (You didn't call it "World War I" until we started "II"). But if I'd had to draw a map of all the world I would have sketched what lay between my father's camp and my grandmother's house. Outside that belt perhaps I would have written, as medieval "mappers" used to do on sections of the world they didn't know, "Here dwell lions."

On the afternoon of Sunday, December 7, 1941, my cousin Jack and I were upstairs in his house, building mansions out of children's wooden blocks. But then my aunt came up and told us that that the Japanese had just attacked us at Pearl Harbor. We gathered this was quite important. But where was this

Pearl Harbor? And what were Japanese? This seemed to be an adults' problem and we found it hard to feel concerned.[4]

Before a year had passed, though, I was tacking stirring posters on my bedroom walls. One of them showed gallant General MacArthur, square-jawed and defiant. Others offered patriotic sayings by American presidents. They glowed in the dark—not, I hope, because they contained radium.

My father served as air raid warden on our street, urging neighbors not to let a ray of light be seen at night in practice bomb alerts. To the disappointment of my friends and me the Germans never flew above and dropped a bomb.

TWO

Hunter of Truth

IN THE FALL of 1943 this was the Big Picture: World War II was beginning its fifth year. Empires were collapsing and the Allies now were on the rise. Scientists were learning to release the energy in atoms.

Meanwhile a boy of twelve was afoot in his own three-billionth share of the world. He was starting adolescence, looking for the "Truth" (or Truths), wondering what girls are all about, and asking himself just who or what he wished to be.

In the fall of 1943 my father started teaching mathematics at The Hill School, a private school for boys in Pottstown, Pennsylvania, outside Philadelphia. (He continued to run Camp Awosting.) So we moved to Pennsylvania, and I skipped the seventh grade and entered "second form" (eighth grade) with the youngest boys at Hill.

The writer Tobias Wolff went to Hill about a decade after I did, and in his memoir, *This Boy's Life,* he writes about the school and those who went there. He says the school's alumni magazine was "filled with pictures of Gothic-style buildings on emerald lawns, big trees in autumn color, playing fields, and the boys themselves. . . . The students looked different from the boys I knew. It wasn't just a difference of clothes and hair style. The difference was tribal—bones, carriage, a signature set of expressions."

For any "new boy" at The Hill School, new-boy cap upon his head, prep school life was strange. We were grouped in "forms," not grades, and taught by "masters," not by teachers. As the word implies, the "masters" all were men, addressed as "sir." We went to chapel nearly every evening, twice on Sunday. On weekdays we wore sport coats and on weekends gray or dark blue suits. In the long, wide dining room, we younger boys sat at tables near the entrance, but each year after that we'd sit at tables nearer to the farther end, where senior masters and the lofty sixth formers sat.

The discipline was fairly strict. For minor crimes like lateness the dean assigned you "marks," and you worked them off by raking leaves. For ghastly ones, like smoking, he handed out demerits, and if you gathered fifty "Ds" the school expelled you. Boys who didn't like the school would make a point of earning 50 Ds. I seldom committed even petty crimes, and I feared that other boys would view me as a teacher's pet, because I was a master's son. So once I went to dinner late on purpose and I asked the master of my table to be sure to report me. He did.

We were allowed to leave the campus only on Wednesday afternoons, when we could walk downtown and savor Pottstown's tepid charms. (In Pottstown "downtown" is known as "uptown," even though it lies where rivers meet.)

The masters had high teaching standards. My Latin teacher often was a trifle tipsy but he was wide awake when we recited. He listened with his head a-tilt, the way a robin does when hunting worms. My French instructor made us learn our drills so well that decades later I could still recite them to him: "*J'entre dans la salle de classe. Je regarde autour de moi. . . .*" ("I enter the classroom. I look around . . .") Their classes, true, were sometimes dull. I still possess a Hill School textbook in which the previous owner had written on the inside of the cover, "I wish the bell [that ended classes] would ring."

Among the masters was of course my father, and in my first year at The Hill School I was in his class, the only one, in algebra. Because I'd skipped a grade, and also since I wasn't good at math, he nearly had to flunk me in the fall. (After that I did a little better.) He was lively, and would hurl an eraser at a boy whose mind was elsewhere. He might even seize an offender by the collar and punt him out the door. In fun. Sam Gwynne, a classmate at The Hill, later told me that in his geometry class my father would remark, "Any damned fool can understand that, right, Gwynne?"

It's strange, given how I later earned my living, but I didn't take to history while at Hill. The master in a course in U.S. history said he liked to read my essays on exams because I thought like an historian. But when I won, for "excellence in French," the shortened version of Toynbee's *Study of History*, I found it dull and didn't read it.

Naturally, what I learned in class was only part of all I learned at Hill. As well as teaching me a lot of English, French, and Latin; a fair amount of history and science; and just a little math (it wouldn't stick), The Hill School made me more aware of money, i.e., wealth. I'd known for years that some folks have it while the others don't, but now I really did absorb that fact.

Among the many wealthy boys at Hill School was my pleasant roommate in our senior year, Lionel Pincus. He was always finely dressed, and so considerate that it wasn't till our class's fiftieth reunion that he mentioned to me casually that my father once had failed him in a math course. I asked him what it had been like to be a Jewish boy at Hill, and he said that sometimes other boys were indirectly rude. Lionel did well without the math my father hadn't taught him; he later founded Warburg Pincus, one of the world's biggest "private equity investors."

Another friend was Isaac ("Tommy") Thomas, a quiet gnome and the biggest "brain" I've ever known. Like my father, Tommy's father also was a master, so we two knew each other well. I'm pretty sure his final grade in every course he took in five

years at The Hill was 1. A 1 was higher than A–; it was equal
to an A or A+. (In five years at The Hill I never earned a 1.)
Among our classmates Tom was famed for having said in an
English class that someone in a novel we had read was "imper-
vious to suggestion."

If a Hill School student wasn't rich and pleasant, like Lionel, he might be smart, like Tommy, and if he wasn't smart it
helped to be an athlete. I recall another classmate, a gifted running back, and how his legs would churn when he was dashing
through the line. It was said that after a dance weekend at Hill
he wrote his date a letter mentioning some doings on a couch,
and that her mother found the letter.

I made my share of gaffes. For example, at a prom I much
admired another student's pretty date, so I learned what school
she went to and I wrote her. This silly girl informed the boy
and after that, any time when we were in a place where other
boys could hear, he hooted at me.

Once I quarreled with a classmate and he shoved me. I protested, using words I must have picked up from a gangster
movie: "Take your greasy paws off me!" I really said that. The
upshot was a fight with boxing gloves before a little crowd. We
fought three rounds and ended with a draw.

AT THE BEGINNING of this chapter I said that as a boy
I wanted to discover what was True. The point is that I did
believe in Truth. I don't mean simply telling truth, small *t*,
because I did and do believe that when we can we ought to tell
the truth. (Of course we shouldn't if the truth is no one else's
business, or will do more harm than good.)

No, this is what I mean by searching for the Truth. As long as
I was at The Hill, and later for a while in college, I thought that
there were never-changing TRUTHS that flared like torches

and could light our paths through life. The Hill encouraged that belief in Truth; its motto, taken from a letter Paul wrote to some Christian converts, is "Whatsoever things are true."

Somewhere, I was certain, were the Answers to life's Questions. One who searched could find those Answers, learn those Truths regarding God, Morality, "the Good," and . . . things like that. I'm something of a reader, so I thought that if I read the proper books I'd find the Answers. In my fifth form year at Hill I somehow got a list of famous essays, treatises, histories, and novels that students read in "Great Books" courses at some colleges and universities, and I set out to devour these Greats. I meant to find the Answers, but I never read beyond the novels.

IN MY SENIOR YEAR at Hill I applied for admission both to Oberlin College, in Ohio, and to Princeton. I couldn't not apply to Princeton. My father and my mother's brother both had gone there nearly 40 years before, and my older brother Bill, whose college education had been delayed by taking part in World War II, was a Princeton sophomore at the time. And many of my Hill School classmates were applying there.

Compared to Princeton, Oberlin was, as Italians say (I don't know why), "another pair of sleeves." Maybe no one from The Hill had ever gone there but I knew that Oberlin was good, and called "the Swarthmore of the Middle West." I also knew the students there weren't only boys, and that was an exciting thought. I also knew that Oberlin was in the U.S. "Heartland," where I'd never been. Perhaps the time had come to see it.

Since Oberlin and Princeton both accepted me, offering modest scholarships, I had to make a choice. At just this time the senior prom at Hill took place. While dancing with a girl from New York City (that fact is relevant), I mentioned that I had to choose between these first-rate, very different institutions. This was her amazed response: "What! Not go to Princeton?"

That decided it. Along with 21 other Hill School classmates (including James A. Baker III, future U.S. Secretary of State) I started Princeton in the fall of 1948. The fact that Princeton took a seventh of my Hill School class suggests that it was not as choosy in the '40s as we acceptees liked to think.

You could almost say that at Princeton I hadn't even left The Hill, since in my first two years I shared a suite of rooms with Hill School classmates. One of them, Jay Sherrerd, later made a heap of money and gave it to The Hill School, Princeton, and a lot of other causes. Joe Bolster later fathered 14 children and in his spare time made his living raising funds for Princeton. Eric Merrifield, whom at Hill we had voted the second "Most Gentlemanly" (and why not first?), became a doctor and ran a hospital. In our sophomore year we added Rich Megargee, a pleasant fellow (we forgave him for not having gone to Hill), who later on became, like me, an historian.

How I did like Princeton! Simply to be free to leave the campus, walk across the street, and buy a cup of coffee was elating. (That's a thing you'll never understand unless you went to prison or to prep school.) But it wasn't just the freedom. It was beer in pitchers, pretty girls with yellow mums at football games, argyles and gargoyles, showboating professors, and Albert Einstein, who lived in Princeton and often walked down Nassau Street. (Or so they say. It happens that I never glimpsed this man whom *Time* would one day name the greatest person of the 20th century.)

It's true that Princeton does produce a lot of silly sentimentality. There's a joke that goes, "How many Princetonians does it take to change a light bulb?" "Three. One to screw the new bulb in and two to stand around and reminisce about how great the old bulb was."

Among the showboating professors was "Buzzer Hall," in History. He was colorful, but (others won't agree) he really didn't teach too well. A verse about him in Princeton's "Faculty Song" proclaims: "On Garibaldi's life and death / He yells himself quite out of breath." (It's said that the tune of the "Faculty Song" was stolen from a Scottish ditty, "The Muckin' o' Geordie's Byre," which means "The Cleaning of the Dung from George's Cowshed.")

Instead of fraternities, Princeton had 17 "clubs," and many clubs had lordly names like Prospect, Ivy, Tower, Terrace, Cap and Gown, and Court. Halfway through my sophomore year I joined Cloister Inn. A Cloister member later invited certain other members to meet with him and talk about what he believed were needed changes in the club. He started out, "I've called this meeting of the better element . . ." Two friends of mine were also there and we promptly named ourselves "The Better Element."

Along with many virtues Princeton had a darker side: It sometimes made us well-intentioned snobs. Our luck in having "advantages" had helped to shape our point of view. Half of us had gone to prep schools like The Hill, and many others were the products of the public schools of wealthy suburbs. We had won admission to the Ivy League, and now we lived in handsome more-Gothic-than-Gothic dorms where others— whom we scarcely noticed—made our beds. In classes we discussed the weekly readings with professors who respected, so we fancied, what we had to say.

We knew the proper clothes to wear, from neck to toes, for big events: tweed sport coat, shirt with buttoned-down collars,

College boy

rep-striped silken tie, gray flannel pants, and dark brown cor-
dovan shoes. And maybe argyle socks.

Despite our unconscious snobbery, if snobbery's the word,
at least in theory we opposed outright exclusion. Here is an
example. Usually, most sophomores received "bids" to join the
eating clubs, but for those who didn't this rejection could be
awful. In our sophomore year our class made Princeton history when three quarters of us signed a pledge that none of us
would join a club till every sophomore got a bid. One day in
March of 1950 *The Daily Princetonian* bore a banner headline:
"ALL SOPHS GET BIDS."

I LIKE AN INSCRIPTION carved in stone on a Princeton
classroom building that begins: "Here we were taught by men
and gothic towers . . ." (Female professors hadn't yet appeared.)

On the whole I liked my courses, which provided moments I will not forget. With other students in a psychology course I visited the state "asylum" for the insane and found the troubled patients riveting. (But I later took my sport coat to the cleaner's, thinking that it smelled of urine.) In a course in Chinese art the professor set some priceless ancient bronzes right before us on the table. And I took some not-for-credit sculpture classes whose notorious attraction was the female models, who were nude.

My grades were not too great. Because of laziness or too much writing for *The Prince* I didn't study hard. My average grade, converted out of Princeton's system into letters, was a mediocre B, and had I not had first-rate training at The Hill it might have been much lower. In the field of history, which in later life would be my career, my grades were less than good. In the European history survey course I took in freshman year my grades were the equivalents of B– in the fall and C in spring.

However, in that survey course we read a little book that had a big effect on me. This was Henri Pirenne's *Economic and Social History of Europe in the Middle Ages*. Does that title sound a trifle dry? The book was not. Pirenne's account of Europe's slow decline when pirates ruled the seas and how it later rose as fairs and peddlers woke it up enthralled me. I still possess my copy of that book.

Although I liked my courses, *The Daily Princetonian,* which appeared each day from Monday to Friday, was my Princeton home. As early as I could in freshman year I "heeled" for the *Prince,* and during my first two and a half years at Princeton I spent a lot of time writing stories for the paper and sometimes editing. Among the other *Prince* reporters was my friend Don Oberdorfer, who later was the diplomatic correspondent of *The Washington Post.*

Once I wrote a lengthy story about a well-known black man, singer/actor Paul Robeson, who had grown up in the town of Princeton. I also wrote about an alumnus who had vanished after the alumni Reunions the previous June and whose body was found in winter when children who were skating on a nearby lake saw his car beneath the ice. And I wrote about a Princeton professor who, at a party at his house, played his final game of Russian roulette.

Halfway through my junior year I realized that I must earn better grades, so I quit the *Prince*. I felt a little guilty; I was letting down some friends who needed all the help that they could get to put a paper out five days a week.

One result of quitting was that I had the time to write a decent senior thesis. I named it *A Poetic for Seventeenth Century Devotional Poetry*. You couldn't say humanity really needed information on that subject.

IN THE MEANTIME, what did I learn about those shining Truths I'd thought about at Hill? Princeton courses seemed to be the place to hunt for Answers.

Well I did run into Questions, even Answers, and I'll tell you some of what I think I learned. You needn't look for brilliant thoughts. This is simply how one ordinary student, busy writing for a campus paper, waiting on tables (to pay for his meals), earning average grades, dating girls, visiting museums, reading novels, taking walks, and chatting with his friends, also searched for Truths.

As I recall, I started out by asking myself, cautiously, if there really was a God. At that time Professor Willard Stace taught Princeton's introductory course in philosophy, and we students used to whisper to each other that this daring British scholar did not believe in God! Certainly his lectures raised my doubts about belief.

I remember very well when Stace, in a lecture, read to us the lines I quote below; no other words have ever seemed to me so grand. Decades later I would write to Stace and ask him for their source, and he answered that Bertrand Russell published them in 1902, in an essay called "A Free Man's Worship."

Here they are:

> Brief and powerless is Man's life; on him and all his race the slow, sure doom falls pitiless and dark. Blind to good and evil, reckless of destruction, omnipotent matter rolls on its relentless way; for Man, condemned to-day to lose his dearest, tomorrow himself to pass through the gate of darkness, it remains only to cherish, ere yet the blow falls, the lofty thoughts that ennoble his little day; disdaining the coward terrors of the slave of Fate, to worship at the shrine that his own hands have built; undismayed by the empire of chance, to preserve a mind free from the wanton tyranny that rules his outward life; proudly defiant of the irresistible forces that tolerate, for a moment, his knowledge and his condemnation, to sustain alone, a weary but unyielding Atlas, the world that his own ideals have fashioned despite the trampling march of unconscious power.

When my brother Bill and I attended church on Easter Sunday in my freshman year the two of us were much surprised to spot Professor Stace amid the congregation.

Princeton then required that freshmen and sophomores go to church, meaning any organized religious meeting, on campus or in town, on half the weekends. If you planned to leave for home on Saturday, you went to a synagogue on Friday. The important thing was the card you signed that proved you'd had your dose of faith. Early in my sophomore year I went to see the dean of the university chapel and asked to be excused from the church-attendance rule.

He did exempt me, but he asked me not to tell my friends, and for decades I supposed that no one else had ever done this daring thing. But when, at last, I told some aged classmates what I did, several of them laughed and told me that they too had had permission not to go to church.

Of course, it wasn't only a philosophy course with Stace that shaped me, and I'd like to think I worked out my ideas myself. However, a course in cultural anthropology, in my sophomore year, nudged me on the road to relativism. This *ism* holds that notions of a god, or what is right and wrong or true and false, aren't absolutes or Truths. Instead, they vary from one culture to another.

I later understood that what we believe may differ not only from one culture to another (who does not know that?) but inside ourselves. That is, we often hold ideas inside us that conflict, that contradict each other. For example, at one time a poll revealed that three out of four Americans believed in the "right to life" (i.e., opposed abortion) while three out of four Americans believed in "a woman's right to choose." We just ignore these contradictions, and perhaps that's just as well. To live with contradictions is the way to save your mind.

I then began to think, and now I'm sure, there are no Answers, only Questions. What philosophy and anthropology began for me, living—merely living—and the study of the past have pushed along. More and more I doubt abstractions. God and Truth are abstractions.

ANOTHER MYSTERY WAS girls. In those benighted years Hill and Princeton both admitted only males, but I did have girl friends, or rather friends who were girls. I sometimes invited them to school and college dances, or to football weekends, and several times these girls invited me to dances or to spend a weekend at their homes. All of them were five feet two, then the statutory height for girls.

The first of them was pretty and straightforward, and after my mother met her she made a point of telling me this girl was nice. She was the first girl that I ever kissed—and just a good night peck at that. However, after my freshman year at Princeton I never gazed on her again, and this is why. In the fall of my sophomore year she wrote inviting me to her college for a football weekend. I had never seen her writing, and was shocked to find it even more childish than mine. Because of that alone I turned her invitation down, saying I was far behind in all my work. Dunderhead! Nincompoop!

The second girl was fun to talk to, and she wore hoop skirts to dances, knitted me a pair of argyle socks in Princeton colors, and taught me how to samba. The last time that I saw her she surprised me with a dumb remark. She said that Jewish students worked too hard, which wasn't fair to others. But I liked her just the same.

The third of them was four years younger than I, and I knew her because for several summers I worked as a cook's helper in a club in the Catskills that my parents managed after they had sold my father's camp. At this club a dozen families owned cottages around a pretty lake, and one of those families was hers. She once invited me to her home for a weekend, so I took a train from Princeton to New York City, a bus to her hometown, and then a taxi to her home. When I rang the bell her mother answered, greeting me with great aplomb. You never would have guessed that this was *not* the weekend they had had in mind.

Later on this girl and I made history of a kind, and several years ago I wrote about it in this letter to the *Princeton Alumni Weekly:*

> Perhaps some alumnus in advanced middle age can answer the question at the end of this letter.
>
> Half a century ago it was not unusual for young women who came to Princeton on weekends to bring along chaperones. . . . [For instance] when my uncle invited a Bryn Mawr student to

Princeton, in 1912, his mother (my grandmother) came along to see that there was no hanky-panky.

Half a century later, in 1951, I invited a high school senior to Princeton for a football weekend. Her mother gave her permission, on condition that her daughter come with a chaperone. So she did. The chaperone kept mostly to herself. . . .

Was I the last Princetonian to have a date come to Princeton with a chaperone?

Soon I heard from an alumnus who had graduated two years after I did. He wrote that once he'd had a date who came to Princeton with a woman who accompanied the girl only as far as the campus, and then went away. Since that is not a chaperone, the answer to the question that I asked at the end of my letter may be "Yes."

MEANWHILE, I SLOWLY learned to write in simple prose. This would be important. Later, in and outside my career, writing mattered to me very much.

That interest had begun in school. At The Hill I wrote a lot of weekly "themes" for English courses, and articles for our weekly paper. Once I took the train to Philadelphia and interviewed a well-known tennis player, Donald Budge, for the *News*.

On the whole I learned to write by doing, but I did absorb some lessons from my teachers at The Hill. Here's a small example. Our English teacher (master) told us that *The New York Herald Tribune* (which still was extant then) allowed a well-known columnist to disobey the paper's rule for commas used with words in series. Other reporters had to list things this way: "peaches, pears and plums"; but Franklin P. Adams was allowed to use a comma after the next-to-last item, like this: "peaches, pears, and plums." I believed you need the "F.P.A. comma" to be clear, and I've used it ever since.

This teacher also had us read some essays by the 17th century philosopher Francis Bacon. He admired Bacon's majestic sentences. Here is an example, one of 65 in my *Oxford Dictionary of Quotations:* "Reading maketh a full man; conference a ready man and writing an exact man." However, when I tried to write like that I found that what had flowed for Bacon lurched for me. I'm sure my classmates found the same. As it happens, four years later someone put these words beneath my picture in our graduation yearbook: "Reading maketh the man. —Francis Bacon." (You'll notice he misquoted.)

All of us reporters, first at Hill and later on at Princeton, liked writing that was "punchy." And it's true that words of a single syllable, if you find the right ones, are the best. What could be more punchy than Irving Mills' "It don't mean a thing if it ain't got that swing"?[1] Would this wording be more effective: "It doesn't signify anything if it doesn't have the necessary rhythm"?

Mort Meyer, a fellow *Prince* reporter, once phoned a story about a thrilling Princeton-Yale basketball game from New Haven (home of Yale) to Princeton. Excitedly he started out, "Give me some words!" The reporter on the telephone at the *Prince* who was taking down Mort's story thought this sentence was the lead, so the story in the *Prince* next day began, "Give me some words!" Now *that* was punchy, though fortuitous.

When I entered Princeton I believed that if there was a single thing that I did well it was writing. So I was shocked and humbled, in my freshman year, when Professor Maurice Kelley didn't like a paper I had written for his course. He even suggested that I take a course in composition. I didn't follow his advice, but in the next three years I did write reams of other papers, and heaps of stories for the *Prince,* and my writing did improve. The same Professor Kelley who had hadn't liked my freshman paper supervised my senior thesis and he clearly liked it. Later he wrote recommendations for me when I applied to grad schools, and . . . we'll see.

WHILE AT PRINCETON I considered several kinds of work. My friend Tim Mutch and I talked lightly of apple farming in the West. We said we'd lay two roads across our ranch at right angles, named Tim Street and Jim Street. For a while I also thought of building houses, forgetting that I couldn't even work a slide rule.

Most of all I dreamed about reporting for a paper, and therefore in the spring of my sophomore year I walked into the city room of *The Newark Star-Ledger*. This was then a wretched rag, a fact that gave me hope that they would hire me for the summer. I told the editor that I'd take any job, even sweeping floors. With just the slightest smile he told me that the sweeping job was filled, but he later wrote and offered me a job as what you might describe as cub reporter. He didn't say so but he wanted an under-paid and after-hours reporter just in case there ever was a major nighttime story and no one else around to cover it.

So in June and July of 1950 I stayed at my Hartwell cousins' house in nearby Orange (beside the house where I had lived until the age of 12) and worked as a reporter for the *Ledger*. I came to work most days at five, when nearly all the other scribes were leaving. But luckily (I guess) no disaster happened; Yankee Stadium did not burn down, nor Newark's City Hall blow up. So I mostly sat at someone's desk and read the novels for a course I planned to take at Princeton in the fall. A red-haired copy girl named Rita Cohen fetched us beer from bars, and I learned that I couldn't write if I had drunk a quart of beer.

When the Korean War began in June the *Ledger* had me go with a photographer to a busy nearby street, stop some pretty girls, take their pictures, and ask them whether women should be drafted for the war. The editor liked my story and the headline I suggested: "Let George Do It!" But when he saw the photos of the girls he called across the city room in great disgust, "Don't you Princeton guys know what a pretty girl is?"

One night the *Ledger* sent me to Newark's railroad station, where someone had been stabbed. The station was empty and eerie, but I found a trail of blood that led from a remote upstairs platform to a first floor office where the injured man had gone for help. Then I went back to the *Ledger,* where I wrote and handed in my story. The editor said, "Wait, a second. Is the victim colored?" "Yes," I answered. "Well," he said, "then we won't use this."

The *Ledger* wasted not a penny. According to a legend, a former publisher, after checking his accounts, stormed into the city room one day. He stretched an arm out and he shouted, "Everybody on this side of the room is fired! Get out!" This cheapness must have won results because in time the *Ledger*'s much-respected rival, *The Newark Evening News,* would close its doors. The *Ledger* then improved and now is Jersey's leading paper.

I noticed the *Ledger* reporters' boredom, and in time I came to understand the reason for it: Many stories were the same as what they wrote the day before. A fire is just a fire. I decided that I didn't want to do this for a living.

Maybe I was wrong. I sometimes think just possibly I might have made a living after college writing feature stories for some lofty paper like *The New York Times.*[2]

A fantasy: Again I'm writing for the *Prince,* but now I'm a feature-story writer who's encouraged, since the other guys all know I'm good, to write about whatever piques my interest. Twice a week I write about such things as whether our professors' research serves a purpose, what our country's fighting for in South Korea, or whether women over 30 all wear girdles. I get my facts right, and my sources tell me things they'd never tell another soul. I write with wit and lots of PUNCH. Everybody reads my column, which I've labeled "Fact." Word about my talent reaches an important person at *The New York Times*. . . .

I ONCE WENT through our graduation yearbook jotting down my classmates' more engaging nicknames. Or what they claimed were their nicknames. They were Fuzzy, Pie, Doc, Mutt, Frog, Nig, Chips, Crankshaft, Wimpy, Muff, Dizzy, Squalid, Bones, Skip, Sack, Bruiser, Punchy, Dad, Go, Jocko, Ape-neck, Goose, Boom-Boom, McGoo, Zero, Wrong-man, Tub, Gink, Nails, Gloom, Poss, Root, Peaches, Bean, Prince, Rags, Spook, Colonel, Skin, Fat Sad, Slut, Sharpster, Monster, Scrote, Booger, Gooker, Cookie, Bird-dog, Woof, and Windy. (The last of these was Windsor Cousins III, who's been my friend for fifty years.)

Ever since my Princeton years the thing I really wanted when I took a wife or found a job or wrote a book was the (imagined) good opinion of such guys as Dizzy, Slut, and Mutt. I didn't know a lot of them and they did not know me, and yet I wanted their approval. It's something I cannot explain.

THREE

Cold Warrior

WHEN I GRADUATED from Princeton in 1952 America was deeply involved in the Cold War and had been fighting in Korea for two years.[1] I knew the Army lay in waiting so I made it easy for them and enlisted on the day after we graduated.

Until then I'd made a series of easy, natural moves from one nourishing institution to another: from home to my father's summer camp for boys to The Hill School and to Princeton. Would the Army be a turning point?

I went through basic training near Washington, D.C. I recall piss-yellow P.X. beer, and a jukebox endlessly whining a song we soldiers loved, "I'd Walk a Mile for a Smile from My Momma and Daddy." Because I'd been an English major, the Army trained me as a combat engineer.

We learned at first to shoot with M1 rifles and later how to build a bridge and how to blow one up. We marched from our barracks to the rifle range to where we built our bridges chanting, "LEFT! LEFT! Your face is red and your pants are tight. / Your balls are swinging from LEFT to RIGHT."

After basic training I went to a "leadership school" which was intended to train us either to be noncoms or to go to Officers Candidate School. There were 24 trainees in our class, mostly with at least a year or two of college. One of them was James P. Becker, a Notre Dame alum who saw the funny side of Army life. (Especially the sergeants.) Jim would be a long-time friend.

Our sergeants trained us to use the bayonet by having each of us in turn run twenty yards and stab a straw-filled dummy. As we ran we had to bellow "Bloody guts! Rotten guts! Slimy guts! KILL!" We were told to stab the dummy while scream-ing "KILL!" but as each of us ran and yelled those words he couldn't keep from laughing, and by the time he reached the end he was wobbling so that he could barely prick the man of straw. Our sergeants glowered, grunting "college fucks."

During training I ran into a Princeton classmate who had recently graduated from Officers Candidate School. I asked him, was it hard? No, he said, you range your textbooks on your shelf according to their height, and never crack them; the big thing is to dust them every day. But I decided not to go to O.C.S., even if they'd take a guy whose mind was none too quick and eyes were poor and hearing had been damaged by the crack of rifles on the range.

I guessed that after training they would send me to Korea, where perhaps I'd build a bridge. Or blow one up. But an Army friend, a clerk, saw my orders and he told me that Jim Becker and I were headed to a city named Trieste. So I looked it up. As perhaps you know, Italy is shaped like a boot. Well, Trieste is at the top of the boot, at the back, where you'd grab the boot if you picked it up. At the time though, Trieste and its hinter-land were a "free territory," with Italy to the west and what was then Yugoslavia to the east. The free territory was the area on the map that runs southeast from Monfalcone.

How did it happen that out of 24 men in our leadership school class they had chosen both the Jims for Trieste? I would bet an Army clerk had picked the two of us for no better rea-son than that alphabetically our surnames, Becker and Davis,

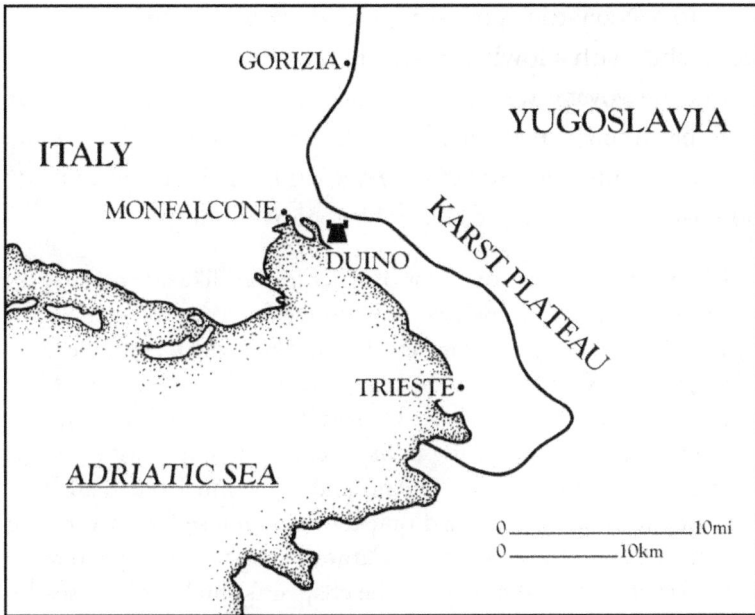

Trieste and its neighbors

topped the availables on our class's muster roll. (Carpenter went somewhere else.) In my case, it may have been that chance event that led to . . . well, you'll see.

BEFORE WE LEFT America, Jim and I stenciled our names on our duffle bags and made inquiries about Trieste. We discovered that the U.S. soldiers who had served there liked the place. Especially they liked the women. A sergeant who had been there told us dreamily that gorgeous, pleasure-loving girls abounded on the beaches by the sea. I've read the memoirs of an American who served there shortly after World War II. He especially recalled "big-titted easy girls."[2]

Along with the new Trieste commanding general, a lot of officers, and perhaps 150 plain GIs, Jim and I embarked for

Italy in a Navy transport ship, the *Private William Thomas*. A troop ship with a lowly private's name?

On the voyage we met Tom Boyd, who rounded out what soon became a threesome. Decades later Tom would write his memoirs, called *A Bowl of Cherries*, and this is his account of how we met and landed easy jobs aboard the ship:

> I happened to open the door of what looked like a broom closet and discovered two soldiers huddled inside, trying to keep out of sight. They were Jim Davis and Jim Becker, who were to become my best army buddies for the next year or so. The broom closet was actually Jim Davis's office. . . . He had landed himself the cushy job of writing a two-page daily newspaper for the ship's passengers (if troops can be called passengers) and crew. Jim Becker, an Irish Catholic from Boston, had quickly made himself known to the ship's chaplain, a fat, indolent Catholic priest . . . and had offered his services as an altar boy for the chaplain's shipboard masses.[3]

Jim took Tom to Father Madigan, who performed Protestant as well as Catholic services. (Is God aware that Catholic chaplains do that?) The priest made Tom, who could play the organ, his assistant for the Protestant services, playing hymns.

Join the Army (not the Navy), see the world. The *Thomas* stopped (now picture this) at Naples, Italy; then Piraeus, Greece, the port of Athens; and then at Istanbul, in Turkey. The rumor was that we went to Istanbul, 800 miles out of our way, to deliver a general's refrigerator. Only after that diversion did the *Thomas* turn around and take us to Trieste. It's true though that it was good for all of us GIs to see those ancient cities (Naples, Athens, and Istanbul). For a future historian like me the opportunity was priceless.

When we stopped at Naples, Army buses took us soldiers on a visit to Pompeii. Among us was a loud GI who came from somewhere in the South. As we drove along, our Italian guide frequently called attention to the blocks of buildings U.S. bombs had smashed in World War II. When we reached Pompeii and left our buses, and we looked down on the famous ruins, this southerner proclaimed, "Shee-it, we sho' bombed the hell out of this place!"[4] As we wandered through Pompeii, our Italian guide took care to show our mostly adolescent group a "cock-'n-balls," carved in an ancient paving stone, that once had pointed to a brothel.

In his memoirs Tom relates this tale concerning Istanbul, and I hope you won't believe a word of it. By the time we got there, so he writes, Tom and Jim and I were out of money but we craved a well-cooked meal. As we left the ship we met a "walking shop," a Turkish peddler whose stock was fastened to the inside of his coat. He told us that he wanted to acquire new goods, so back to the ship we went. We stripped the sheets from other soldiers' bunks, and Jim and I wound Tom in these and helped him stretch his coat around them. Then we hustled Tom, so padded he could barely walk, past the sentry and down the gangplank to the pier. After Tom unwound we sold the "liberated" sheets to the "walking shop," and then we ate at what Tom said (Tom would know) was Turkey's finest restaurant.

WHEN AT LAST the *Thomas* reached Trieste and docked, I saw a handsome 19th century port. The hills that ringed the city then were green, not concrete gray. I seem to remember that as we stood there on the deck, a hundred yards from shops and small cafés, I smelled the splendid coffee of Trieste and not-so-splendid "Nazionali" cigarettes.

Let me summarize some history. (See the map on page 39.) Decades earlier, after World War I, the Austro-Hungarian Empire had split apart and Italy got the empire's busy southern port, Trieste. In World War II, however, Italy had fought on the losing side, while partisans in Yugoslavia (which by then was Trieste's eastern neighbor) had fought beside the Allies. So who should get the city now, Italy or communist "Yugo"?

This wasn't just a European problem. Beginning shortly after World War II the "West," led by America, and the communist world, led by Russia, were engaged in a nearly world-wide Cold War. So when both sides took an interest in the fate of Trieste—who would get it?—it became a global problem. American and British troops were stationed in Trieste to keep its neighbors from grabbing the city and its hinterland until the major powers decided what to do about it.

Meanwhile, life for Triestines was hard. They were known for noise and cheer, but Trieste was still recovering from World War II, and in the early 1950s it was worn and poor. Workers swept the streets with brooms of bundled twigs, and poor men picked up butts of cigarettes to smoke. Cars were still uncommon, and many people rode to work on noisy motorbikes. They often drove behind our trucks, closer than was wise, risking all for shelter from the "Bora," Trieste's famous winter wind.

What we GIs were going to notice most about Trieste was girls. What we had heard about them before leaving America was, in a word, true. I would write my parents that the "girls are about 100% prettier than the girls in the United States and about 200% better shaped." Each of them owned one stylish, stunning tailored dress or suit, and beauteous blondes cashiered in shops, seated by the windows where the passersby could ogle.

I hadn't any notion what this pleasant city had in mind for me.[5]

Buses took us to a crumbling ex-hotel for a two-week "orientation." As usual in the Army, barbers hacked our hair and officers gave warnings. Since we were front-line soldiers in the

Cold War (so they said) they stressed the need to stay away from COMMUNISTS and BAD WOMEN, warning that we might meet women who were *both* COMMUNISTS *and* BAD. To avoid these perils we should stay away from places marked with circled Xes (thus: ⊗) and the words "Off limits."

They told us that our mission was to keep both Italy and Yugoslavia from seizing Trieste. What made that hard to understand was what we did and didn't know about those countries. Though Italy had been an enemy in World War II that really didn't matter to us. We viewed it as a friendly land from which many immigrants had come to America. I remembered the "Italians" I had known as a small boy in Orange, New Jersey: Tulio, Rocco, Dodo, and a lot of kids in school. I saw Italy as the home of Leonardo and Michelangelo, as well as movie stars like lovely Lollobrigida and magnetic Mastroianni.

Yes, Yugoslavia had been our friend in war. But it was less familiar and its government was communist, though not in Russia's heavy style. Yugoslavia's border, only a few miles inland from Trieste, was part of the "Iron Curtain" that split the "Free World" from the other.

AFTER BEING ORIENTED, the "grunts," the soldiers who would really fight in case of war, moved to barracks on the Carso, also known as the Kras or Karst, the rugged, rocky plateau above the city. There they'd spend their days in training, and I'll bet they also couldn't wait to find BAD WOMEN. But the Army had decided I should be a clerk, so they took us desk combatants to the place where we would live. This turned out to be a villa near the city that, a mere eight years before, had housed the Nazi police. A concrete bunker filled its small front yard.

My job at first was typing forms, but I was judged incompetent at this, even by the Army's not exacting standards. Perhaps

I had exaggerated my typing skill. The officer in charge demoted me to running a mimeograph machine, which used a spinning stencil to make copies of written orders. But I proved to be a greater bungler with the stencils than the forms.

Meanwhile Jim Becker had found a job as sports reporter for *The Blue Devil,* the weekly Army newspaper, and he told the captain in charge of the paper about me. The captain invited me to join the paper as a reporter, and I was happy to accept. I was pleased about my change of job, and so perhaps was the lieutenant for whom I first had hunted-and-pecked and later ruined stencils. When I left he shook my hand and wished me well, looking cheerful.

I moved to the villa above the city where we reporters and also our radio-announcer colleagues slept. Then I started work in *The Blue Devil's* two crowded rooms in a building that housed Trieste's main newspaper. Meanwhile Tom Boyd left his job as a chaplain's assistant and became a radio announcer, so Becker, Boyd, and I were all together.

You couldn't say that we reporters worked too hard. Our editor, a Regular Army sergeant, used to phone the bar across the street from time to time and order rum and Cokes. A waitress brought him singles on Mondays and Tuesdays, doubles on Wednesdays and Thursdays, and triples on our busy Fridays, when we put that week's *Blue Devil* to bed.

If our editor didn't drive himself too hard, neither did we. Each of us half dozen reporters could have done his week's "work" in a day. Once or twice a week I'd phone the motor pool and get a jeep and local driver so that I could gather news. This man would drive me to various Army offices and to the command's headquarters in Miramar Castle. It was fun to drive through Slovene-speaking hamlets on the Carso. The driver and I would sometimes stop at village taverns for a little wine.

We reporters were required to go to work on Saturday mornings, and we resented this. Since the paper had appeared on Friday there was nothing to do on Saturday. So we made a point of doing nothing.

Our officers were very cautious about what they let us print in the paper. Our lieutenant colonel, a West Pointer whom we rarely saw, once clarified this point for me: The Army's mission trumps the truth, he said, and our mission as reporters was not to state the facts but to keep the military locomotive rolling. Mere facts might hurt the troops' morale and give "the Communists" information they could use.

In civilian life our captain, the man who'd rescued me from tearing stencils, had been the editor of a magazine called *Gags*. Since he dreaded going back to that career, he was careful not to make mistakes. He showed up in our office every Friday after lunch, as we saw the paper through the press, and from there he phoned the colonels to ensure that what we planned to print wouldn't get him into trouble.

A good example of what *The Blue Devil* could not report on were "maneuvers." Once a year, in spring, the whole command spent several days "in the field" on the Carso. Several thousand grunts, the real ones from the barracks, pretended to make war, while clerks and scribes like me would sit in tents pretending we were doing what we always did. These maneuvers were a big event for all GIs, and every Triestine was well aware that they were going on. But we couldn't even mention them in *The Blue Devil*.

I DIDN'T KNOW IT, but I was easing into what was going to be my calling.

For one thing, I was learning to speak another language, in addition to the French (and Latin) I had learned in school. I was keen to learn. When barely off the ship I wished a police-man "Buona sera!" (good evening) and was pleased to hear him answer with the same. Even in the first weeks on *The Blue Devil*, when I knew at most two dozen words of Italian, I already served as the interpreter between us American reporters and Peppi and Toni, the Triestine compositors who put *The Blue Devil* together. I learned Italian that way, and from hearing it in movies, and from chatting with the drivers of the Jeeps. And I even paid for lessons. My teacher and I read *Pinocchio*, which he used because it's written in such simple words. It starts, "Once upon a time there was ... A king, my little read-ers will say. No, children, you are wrong. There was once a piece of wood."

I was thrilled when a secretary I talked to by phone thought she was speaking to another Triestine. And delighted when a policeman saw me jay-walking and reproved me *in Italian*. I was in civilian clothes and he never guessed that I was not a Triestine.

However, I wasn't starting my career in history only by learn-ing a language. There was also travel. Because Italy was still recovering from the war the prices weren't too high, and our Army pay went far. I traveled cheaply all the way from Venice in the north to Capri in the south.

Often on a weekend I would take the train to some tour-isty Italian town. The first of these was Venice, which I later came to know so well. Soon after my first arrival there I lost my way, as every tourist in that city does, and, wandering through an archway, I first saw St. Mark's Square. That's the way to see that famous place, which Napoleon once said was Europe's finest drawing room. Stumble on it, find it by sur-prise. At the farther end was stunning St. Mark's Basilica. Mark Twain once wrote that the great church looked like a warty toad out for a walk, but even famous writers sometimes get things wrong.

In several towns I saw the paintings I had studied while at Princeton. As I've said, I'm not religious, but the paintings I loved most were Giotto's frescoes of the life of Jesus, which cover nearly all the walls and ceiling of a little church in Padua. A fresco near the door provides a glimpse of Middle Ages social history. It shows the wealthy moneylender who built the church presenting a model of it to Mary, Jesus's mother. He had probably built the church to make amends for the sin of lending funds at interest. Otherwise he'd spend eternity in Hell.

An Army friend and I took a two-week furlough, with plans to see a lot of Italy. First we went to Venice, where by chance (or so he said) we met an American girl he knew. She was with a female college friend and they had a rented car, so we traveled with them all the way from Venice southward to the island of Capri and north again to Florence. We saw the usual striking things including St. Peter's Cathedral and the catacombs in Rome, and Michelangelo's David in Florence. At Capri a handsome young Italian who rowed us to the Blue Grotto asked us if we knew "Cookie from Vassar."

All this sightseeing raised my interest in Italian history. Here's the kind of thing I mean: In Bologna once I noticed that a lot of bullet holes pocked the stone around a window. I looked across the street, and there as well the stone around a window had been pocked. It wasn't hard to figure out that during World War II men had shot at one another here.

In October 1953, Britain and the United States announced their plan to pull their soldiers from Trieste and hand the city back to Italy. As a result, pro- and contra-Italy students and other Triestines rioted for several days, and six young

Triestines were shot to death. The world was watching on that infant medium, television.

One day while these riots were occurring, several of us reporters and radio announcers were assigned to guard the Army radio station building in Trieste. We were posted in each window holding carbines, but our carbines *were not* loaded. A major told us that only if the matter turned extremely grave would he give us pencil-pushers bullets. When our captain (formerly of *Gags*) saw Boyd he handed him a rifle, bayonet, and helmet. But Tom informed the captain he was on his way to lunch, and he got inside his Topolino (Mouse), and drove away.

From the window I was guarding I couldn't see Trieste's main square, where demonstrations were occurring. But I could hear the rat-tat-tat of rifles while I saw the Triestines—men and women, even babies in their prams—watching grim events as if they were a show put on for their amusement. Repeatedly I saw this crowd surge forward toward the square, run away when they heard firing, halt and gather up their nerve, and once again (with prams) flow toward the square. Peace returned when British and American troops arrived and took control.

Trieste would be a "free territory" until 1954. And what became of Boyd and Becker? Tom broke an ankle skiing, so the Army sent him home. He married and he later moved to England where, for years, purely out of love of music, he has translated operas into English and then produced them. Jim Becker went home, also married, and became a writer and art teacher. Several years ago he died.

I FIRST MET ELDA in a bar. Because that doesn't sound so good, allow me to explain. At one point we reporters and announcers lived in quarters in a former small hotel outside

Trieste. Its name was Bellavista, meaning "pretty view." Sloping down below it was a park, and farther down, beside the sea, was Miramar Castle, the U.S. military headquarters. Maximilian, Archduke of Austria, had built this ersatz castle in the 1850s, but before it was finished he became emperor of Mexico, where revolutionaries killed him. I used to go to the castle once a week because the colonels and the majors might have stories for *The Blue Devil.*

When we reporters and announcers went to live in the Bellavista, the musicians in the Army band, who often played for reviews at the castle, were already living there. These musicians were a vivid lot, earnest when on duty, hip when not. They tied their ties in Windsor knots and called each other "man."

Among the Bellavista's strong points was a snack bar where a guy could buy a burger or a brew. In my first day at the Bellavista I stepped inside this room, guided by a player in the band. He introduced me to a pretty woman behind the bar and told me "This is Elda." I gazed at dark brown eyes, dark brown hair, and a dazzling smile.

Elda Žužek had grown up in the village of Vižovlje (pronounced VEE-zhol-yeh) on the Carso, which I mentioned earlier. The Carso is a land of sinkholes, grottoes, cliffs, and fields of rock. It stretches from above Trieste into what was Yugoslavia then and now is Slovenia. It's the classic example of limestone geology, the one you find in textbooks. When I first saw the Carso it was almost treeless because of sheep- and cattle-grazing and because the farmers burned its saplings in their stoves.

In the map on page 39, Vižovlje is where the I is in "DUINO." It's less than a mile from the Adriatic Sea and nine miles from Trieste. Back then its families numbered just 16, but today it covers all the hill above it.

Vižovlje in 1953

Elda had gone to school nearby until, in 1944, German soldiers burned her village and three others. After that her family shared a little building with two other families until, shortly
after the war, their village was rebuilt. Elda then had worked
as an assistant to two seamstresses in Trieste, and briefly at the
snack bar where we met.

While the people of the city spoke Italian, the people on the
Carso spoke in Slovene, a Slavic language that resembles Russian. Elda had spoken only Slovene till the age of six, when she
started school and was obliged to speak Italian. After that she
was also fluent in Italian as are all the local Slovene people. As
for English, she couldn't say much more than "hahmboorger"
and "donbugme."

As you'll notice, later in these memoirs, the nature of the vil-
lagers' lives was going to be important to me. What struck me
most at first was just how low their living standard was. For an

American it was a shock to see whole villages with little heating and no inside plumbing. Almost no one had a car or phone. The Slovene men I got to know near Elda's village were quarry or shipyard workers who sometimes kept a cow or two. A man with four was viewed as quite well off.

WE DIDN'T FALL IN LOVE at once. But later, after we Americans prepared to leave and the Bellavista had closed down and I was living in the city once again, we saw each other every evening. For Elda this took courage, since a young woman who cared about her reputation did not go out with American (or any other) soldiers. We spoke Italian. I mentioned Elda in a letter home in early October, saying she was "a very dear friend, and I mean it just like that." Of course, that comment caught my mother's eye.

One evening in October Elda looked at me and asked, "What potion have you given me to drink?" She meant, "How did you make me love you?" I answered, "Will you marry me?" It took several minutes for Elda to be sure she understood what I was saying, and certain that I meant it. Then she answered yes.

Everyone who knew us must have thought, and some of them declared, you aren't the same. Can't you see that this won't work?

Both our families were concerned. Not long after she and I became engaged, her parents invited me to their house for dinner. Communication (in Italian, which was not their native tongue nor mine) wasn't easy. Her father said, "We like you, but we can't let Elda marry you." He told me that they didn't want to have her leave and go so far away. I answered mildly that I supposed that that was up to Elda to decide. They may have thought that I was right; they raised no more objections.

I wrote my parents:

I don't know just how to begin or end or fill in the middle of this
letter . . . You may remember that in my last letter I mentioned
briefly a girl who worked in the snack bar at the band where we
live and said that she was a "very dear friend" or something of that
sort. Well, to make a very short story shorter, she and I are in love,
and I have asked her to marry me, and she has said yes.

My father answered, much concerned, suspecting many
things:

Your letter with its great news arrived this a.m. . . . I must in all
honesty mention the cons as well as the pros. . . .

And my mother wrote:

I can only hope with Dad that you have thought your love and
your problems through. [We] cannot but be happy in your happi-
ness and ready to help with your problems.

Tactfully she wrote to Elda:

Just this morning I received Jim's letter with its wonderful news,
and I am delighted to write at once and tell you how delighted
we are. We have wanted a daughter for many years, and now we
are to have one.

Elda's mother wrote my parents in Slovene, and a friend of
hers translated:

We are against the marriage of our daughter to Jim not because of
your son but because of the distance that would have to separate
us. For us all, unfortunately, it is a great sorrow and pain and great
worry for a mother. If the destiny of Elda and Jim is that they love
each other, one must resign oneself to it.

We had a photographer take Elda's picture and sent it to
America. Seeing what she looked like somewhat eased my par-

Elda, 1953

ents' fears, and then we phoned them. Though Elda knew a few words of English, I had written down some phrases she could use. Hearing Elda's pleasant voice meant a great deal to my parents.

I wrote to them:

Her charming face, her mannerisms of speech and facial expression, and her sense of humor are an attractive combination. I remember that [another reporter on *The Blue Devil* remarked some months ago] that perhaps one day one might weary of these qualities in her, but that he could not imagine how. And so it has proved with me.

My father answered:

My dear, dear son Jim: . . . [I was] very doubtfully on the fence up to now, and I think rightfully so. Your letter received today . . . has brought me over to your side. I believe yours to be a real marriage for love.

My brother Dick reassured me:

I don't think you need worry for an instant over the situation.
Your family is with you. . . . I feel I have never been anything but
with you.

Elda wrote a letter to my parents (and a friend of hers
translated):

I write to you in order to thank you for your affection towards
me. . . . I hope that one day not too distant I will also be able to
embrace you and love you as my parents.

And I reported to my parents on the eve of the wedding:

I feel like a man holding his nose and getting ready to jump from
the high diving board. Here goes!

It happened that my mother owned a family diamond, and
she had it mounted in an engagement ring, which she sent me.
Elda and I were married in April 1954 in a village church quite
near her home. Elda wore a long white gown that her former
boss, a seamstress, had confected for her. Since my father still
was teaching at The Hill, my parents couldn't come. My Army
friends arrived at the church at 10, when the wedding was supposed to start, but didn't. That's Italy. Before 11, when the wedding started, most of them had had to leave. That's the Army.

Two *Blue Devil* friends were able to stay for the wedding
and the long reception, and one of them was the paper's photographer. He took a lot of pictures, one of which appears on
the facing page. Elda and I honeymooned in Slovenia, behind
the Iron Curtain.

After I had left for home Elda wrote my parents:

[Jim] has wrote to me a letter from Casablanca [where the troop
ship briefly stopped] and now I must wait before he arrive at
home. Every day is more long for me, to remain alone here.

Newly married

She had to wait for a U.S. visa, so she arrived in America four months after I did.

UNTIL I WAS about to marry and leave the Army and therefore had to think about it in Trieste in the winter of 1954, I had never carefully considered how I'd later earn a living. At different times since childhood I had pictured being a fireman, mineralogist, reporter, doctor, apple farmer, literature professor, and house builder.

In my last months in the Army in Trieste, however, I decided I would earn a Ph.D. in history and become a professor. All the sightseeing that I described above had helped to lead me to this decision, and in a letter to my parents I explained why I would study history. "I would feel that I had a real mission in teaching history. Much that was done wrong in the past was done because people knew nothing of what had been done before them. Someone who would make others aware of these past successes and failures would be doing a real service." I later changed my mind about the reasons one should know about the past.

It was somewhat odd that I should decide to study history, and I'll tell you why. I had sometimes wondered whether I'm the only living human being. The rest of you, I sometimes thought, existed only when you were in my presence. Have you ever had this "only me" belief? If you did you didn't tell a soul. It's known as solipsism, and even now I think it cannot be refuted by logic, but only by common sense. But can you picture someone who isn't sure that all those other people ever lived becoming an historian?

In the evenings, writing on a *Blue Devil* typewriter with a well-worn ribbon, I typed the applications for admission and financial aid to graduate history departments at nine American universities. I told them I wanted to study the history of the Italian Renaissance.

Seven of the nine turned me down, and two said yes but didn't offer money. So in the spring of 1954 I returned from Italy to America, a young man with uncertain prospects.

FOUR

On My Way

WITH MY ARMY SERVICE in Italy behind me I returned to America in May of 1954 hoping to make a career of teaching and writing history. I would do this during decades when American universities and colleges were growing fast and struggling to reconcile two aims: teaching well and adding to the human store of knowledge.

First I had to learn my trade, and that you do in grad school. Elda soon followed me to America, and that made getting on the way, finding a grad school, a pressing need. It was complicated by the fact that in the previous spring seven first-rate history departments had judged my applications for admission and had answered *No*.

The major reason they had turned me down was clear. My grades at Princeton had been barely over average, and, to make things worse, in my senior year I'd failed a philosophy course. I hadn't read the books, perhaps because they didn't interest me. I should have bluffed or hum-bugged on the exam, but I was such a schnook! Instead I'd written in my exam book that I would take my punishment, so the professor flunked me, just as he should have.

All was not lost, however, if I chose to go ahead despite the seven *No*'s. Since I was now a veteran, the

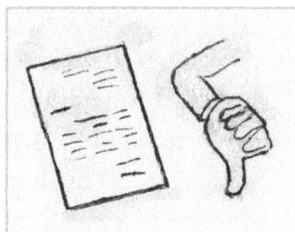

". . . sorry to inform you . . ."
(by JCD)

U.S. government would pay for my tuition and some living costs. This benefit was the well-known "G.I. Bill."

Columbia University's first-rate history department was one of the two that had at least accepted me, although without a fellowship. So my brother Bill and I went to New York to see if Columbia was right for Elda and me. The university's housing office suggested that we look at apartments in a nearby apartment building but when we went to see it a prostitute approached us in the lobby. It looked like this would not work out.

What then? Since Pennsylvania State University had also admitted me, Elda and I went there and I began to work toward a master's degree. I was a former English major switching to history, and when I started I didn't know Adam from atom or Russia from Prussia. But I learned a lot and wrote a thesis on a dismal topic, *The Attitude of Florentines toward Death, 1375–1410*. After a year I had my master's.

My adviser at Penn State counseled me not to continue there for a Ph.D. degree. He said it wouldn't be a "good" degree because it wouldn't help me to land a job, and I hope I thanked him for this frank advice. In the liberal arts Penn State lacked a strong faculty, a first-rate library, and, above all, prestige. So I applied again, as I had done the year before in Italy, to many universities. This time though, a first-rate place, Johns Hopkins, not only admitted me but also offered me a teaching assistantship. What excitement when I read the letter!

And yet I felt a bit uneasy. If I went to Hopkins my adviser there would be Professor Frederic Lane. He was widely known, and his research dealt with the history of Venice, which was fine for me. However, it happened that a young history instructor at Penn State had recently earned his Ph.D. at Hopkins, and he warned me Lane was known to be a bear.

Despite that warning, in the fall of 1955 Elda, our newborn baby David, and I moved to Baltimore.

The Hopkins history department was small but good. Many of our classes met around a seminar table at which (it's said) two famous former Hopkins students once had sat: future President Woodrow Wilson and a well-known historian, Frederick Jackson Turner. Most importantly, I found that Lane was not a bear at all. He was a kindly but demanding scholar, someone you respected and you didn't want to disappoint. If I had an appointment to see him at 11:00, I would stand outside his office door at 10:59, looking at my watch and poised to knock.

For the next two years I was not only a graduate student but also a teaching assistant in a European history survey course. This task was scary since almost the only history that I knew was what I'd learned the year before while at Penn State. I also looked extremely young. Once when three of my students who were Army veterans like me invited me to have a beer with them it was I, their teacher, whom the waitress asked to prove he was of age.

On the first day of classes in my second year at Hopkins I wrote this in my journal:

> One of my students said as he entered the classroom, "Well, sir, who do you want to win today in the World Series?" [I didn't like either the Yankees or the Brooklyn Dodgers so] I said, "Neither, I wish they could beat each other." He turned to a friend and said [maybe smiling], "I don't think I'm going to like this guy."

I also wrote:

> A group of us [second year graduate students] at lunch in the cafeteria had a fine time listing the questions which first-year graduate students always ask, including "How many years will it take me to get through here?"

We old-timers didn't know the answer to that question any more than the new arrivals did. Much depended on the student, but at least five years seemed sure.

DURING MY FIRST YEAR Lane taught a seminar course for two other graduate students and me. Each of us wrote two short papers for him about the elections of some Venetian doges, using what we could learn from a published many-volume diary that a Venetian "noble" kept from 1496 to 1533. Lane devoted one of our seminar meetings to tearing apart the first of my two papers.

In mid-winter I had a talk with Lane over coffee in the cafeteria, and I asked him, "Can I make a go of this? Do I have what it takes?" He said, "I think you have the makings of a good historical writer." I noticed that he didn't say "a good historian."

Of course, I wished to prove, to him and to myself, that I did have what it takes to be an historian. So, near the end of my first year at Hopkins, I wrote a paper about the deeds of a Venetian nobleman named Andrea Gritti, who spied for Venice during a naval war with Turkey. My main source was the diary we had used in the seminar to study doges' elections.

This was Gritti's story: In 1496, when Venetians suspected that the Turks of the Ottoman Empire were planning to go to war against their city-state, Gritti was a Venetian merchant in the grain trade, based in Istanbul, Turkey. He had been there long enough to father three sons by a mistress.

I had seen Istanbul three years earlier when the Army troopship I was on stopped there for a day. (I mentioned this in Chapter 3. This was the occasion when, allegedly, Tom Boyd, Jim Becker, and I stole some sheets from the ship and sold them to a Turk.) Having seen the ancient city now proved useful; I could picture the events involving Gritti that the diary related.

Gritti made himself a spy, and he wrote letters informing the Venetians about Turkish ships and plans, using a simple code based on what he pretended were business events. For example, when he wrote (before the war began) that pirates had captured a 200-barrel merchant ship, the Venetians rightly understood (I don't know how) that the Turkish fleet comprised 200 ships. After the war began the Turks intercepted some of Gritti's letters, saw that he was spying, and jailed him.

When the war was nearly over the Turkish sultan freed Gritti and he returned to Venice, where he helped to negotiate a peace. In the next three decades he served his city-state as both a general and admiral, and near the end of his career his fellow nobles elected him their doge. The Venetian artist Titian painted a splendid portrait of him that hangs today in Washington's National Gallery of Art.

I tried to show how Gritti's career illustrated a pattern that was typical—although he wasn't really typical—of Venetian politicians: first success in business, then in government.

Lane liked my Gritti paper and I think it helped to convince us both that I had a future as an historian. Nearly twenty years later I revised that paper and got it published in an Italian journal, *Studi veneziani.*

BECAUSE I HAD a wife and then a child and then another baby, Daniel, I couldn't dawdle. When I finished my second year at Hopkins the time had come to write a dissertation on some subject in Venetian history. Perhaps you know this: the dissertation is the highest hurdle for the Ph.D.; it's how you prove what you can do.

So now I had to return to Venice and produce a dissertation. I won a Fulbright scholarship, and in the summer of 1957 Elda and I, along with our two boys, returned by ship to Italy. If this was exciting for me it was even more than that for Elda.

She would see her aged parents, whom she'd feared she'd never see again.

At first the four of us all lived in Venice, where I was doing my research. But we found it would be better if Elda and the children stayed in her parents' house outside Trieste. So I rented a room for myself in Venice in a run-down wing of a mansion.

This place was managed by a Scotsman—yes, a Scot in Venice—who had strange beliefs. Since right angles don't exist in nature, he had rounded the corners of his rooms with strips of plasterboard. And because he thought that little boys and girls should not eat meat, since eating flesh destroys our inner angel (bringing out the beast), his children lived on oatmeal, and you could see right through them. On the mantel in the living room was an urn that held the ashes of another child, one perhaps who hadn't thrived on oats.

This man had planned to run a boarding school for English-speaking girls, but girls did not appear and that was why he rented out the rooms. Several of his roomers were unusual. They included a portrait painter who decades later went to prison for "transporting" letters by famous Americans out of the National Archives. Other roomers were a writer of children's books; a woman from the north of England who taught English and became my closest friend; and a recent "Miss Oslo," a pretty blonde Norwegian. When the wife of a prominent Venetian found this girl in bed with her husband some official ordered Oslo out of Venice.

My mind was always on the dissertation. I had thought I might do research on the doughty Gritti, but when I saw his war reports I knew that this was not a good idea. My dissertation would have been an old-style drum-and-trumpet sleeping pill.

After weeks of searching, I found a topic that I liked: the way the ruling class of Venice, over centuries, shrank in number and declined in wealth. The nobility were a closed caste that had almost never taken in new members, as ruling classes elsewhere did. And they didn't want to take them in, not ever. To make sure that no outsider sneaked inside their ranks, they kept good records of their births, marriages, and deaths. These so-called "Golden Books" would be my most important source.

To run their city-state, which included both mainland Italian towns and Mediterranean islands, the nobles needed a core of about a hundred able, wealthy men. Gritti was that kind of man, but more typical of this able core was Leonardo Donà dalle Rose, a dedicated politician about whose family line I would later write a book. Every time Leonardo served in a new post, he began by studying the laws that applied to it, and the reports of his predecessors. He also took the time to train the younger noblemen to run the state. He served as ambassador to Spain and Turkey, and near the end of his career his fellow nobles chose him as their doge.

After 1550, however, three things began to reduce the number of able and wealthy nobles below that needed core of about a hundred. Epidemics of plague killed many nobles, and their new-born custom of limiting the number of their marriages (to avoid dividing family fortunes) had the same effect. (Fewer marriages meant fewer children.) Meanwhile, business opportunities were drying up, and the nobles were getting poorer as well as fewer.

The nobility knew they had a manpower shortage. Half-heartedly, therefore, and complaining about prostituting the nobility, "this unstained Virgin," to the basest kind of people, they finally did admit some other wealthy families to their group. But they did not take in enough, and so they were in trouble when, in 1797, Napoleon conquered Venice, making this wealth-and-numbers problem moot.

With my research done we sailed back to America, and now I had to take the Hopkins final oral examination. I was nervous, and I couldn't say a thing, but the committee of professors from several departments held their noses and approved me. I sent a telegram to Elda, who was staying at my parents' house in Pennsylvania: "PASSED EXAM CALL ME DOCTOR HOME NEXT WEEK."

Counting the time at Penn State, it had taken me five years to earn my Ph.D. degree. And that was fast.

Now I HAD to land a job, and luckily I found a temporary one at Oberlin, of all the college and universities in the world. Twelve years earlier I had chosen not to study at Oberlin, although they'd offered me a scholarship. (You may recall that I was influenced by a girl from New York at a Hill School dance who cried out, "What! Not go to Princeton?" So I'd gone to Princeton.) But now I was to teach at Oberlin, whose history department had hired me as a substitute for a colleague on sabbatical.

Incidentally, in one respect I may have been quite wrong about Ohio. Back when I considered studying at Oberlin, eleven years before, I had thought that it was in the U.S. Heartland. However, when I got there I learned that many Ohioans were surprised if you said that they were living in the Middle West. But were they right? Where exactly is Ohio? Confusingly, my *New American Desk Encyclopedia* calls it an "east north central state of the US Midwest."

Ohio was the birthplace or the home of eight American presidents. They were not our best and not our worst.

Oh no, not our worst.

The history chairman was a nice old fellow who two decades earlier had written a book about Oberlin's early history. I don't know why I did it, since they were only hiring me for a year, but at my interview I asked him whether Oberlin encouraged research. He said the college liked its professors to be "working on" something.

Five out of six of my Oberlin history colleagues had earned their Ph.D.s at Harvard, and they viewed the sixth with scorn because he'd earned his doctorate at Columbia. One of the older professors was surprised to learn that I hadn't earned my Ph.D. at Harvard. He told me that when *he* had served as department chairman he hired instructors by writing to Harvard's history department and taking what they had to offer.

At the end of the year, Oberlin offered me a permanent appointment. In the meantime, though, since they had hired me initially only for a year, I had hunted for another job. The University of Toronto offered me one, but I accepted a job at the University of Pennsylvania. Penn was near my family, something Elda liked as much as I did. And to work there looked quite challenging, since Penn requires research.

Before I left Oberlin I attended the final faculty meeting of the year. The president had recently proposed a major change: that the college drop the two-semester system and switch to the quarter system. If the faculty approved, this measure would very much affect their lives, not to mention those of students. If I had voted, I would have voted yes, but since I was about to leave it seemed unfair to cast a vote, and I didn't. The number of NO votes precisely equaled the number of YESes, so the measure failed. I remember well the look on the president's face.

Just as it had seemed remarkable when Oberlin had hired me, since I might have gone there twelve years earlier as a student, so it now seemed even stranger that Penn had given me a job. Six years before, while in the Army, I had applied to Penn (and eight other places) for admission as a graduate student and for a fellowship. (In effect, admission and a fellowship were linked.) Penn's graduate school dean had sent me this response:

> Dear Mr. Davis,
>
> I am sorry to have to inform you that you were unsuccessful in your application for an award.... Unfortunately, we do not have enough fellowships and scholarships to be able to make awards to all worthy applicants.
>
> Sincerely yours,
> Roy F. Nichols, Dean

He didn't bother to mention that I was also not admitted; that was understood.

But now I was to teach at Penn, and as a colleague of the man who wrote that he was "sorry." Nichols wasn't just a dean but a well-known historian, a winner of a Pulitzer Prize.

In finding a job at Penn I was lucky, though it's true I had competed for it at a time when universities were fast expanding. The demand for academic labor had not only helped me to land a job but would also help me later on to win a permanent Penn appointment. The wind was in my sails.

At the age of 30 I had married, fathered children, earned a Ph.D., and found a job. Were the challenging decades of my life over? Memoirs often end just where the writer seems to have resolved his (or her) problems.[1] So maybe here I ought to write THE END.

Well, I won't.

AFTER OUR DAUGHTER Miriam was born, near the end of our stay in Oberlin, we moved to Philadelphia. There we bought a house on land I later learned had a remarkable link to me. I had known that in the late 1600s my great-great-

great-(pause)-great-great-great-grandfather, Hans Peter Umstatt, had owned land somewhere in the same section of Philadelphia where we now lived. He had bought this holding just before he sailed from Germany to Pennsylvania. But where in Philadelphia was that former Umstatt land? By any chance was it near our house? An archivist at the Germantown Historical Society found a deed that gave the answer: Yes, by extraordinary chance our house was on a little piece of Umstatt's land.

The larger context of all Americans' lives during my first 15 years at Penn was the war in Vietnam, halfway round the Earth. I wrote several letters to newspapers about that great fiasco, which was going to cost, depending on who was counting, at least one and possibly as many as three million lives.

Center City, Philadelphia, as it (more or less) is now (by JCD)

That's if you count the dead Vietnamese, which we Americans tended not to do.

In a letter that *The New York Times* published in 1965 I wrote, "only a total and terribly bloody effort by perhaps hundreds of thousands of United States soldiers could pacify South Vietnam." But I was wrong. We later learned that even half a million of us couldn't do that job.

Americans who thought the war was fine stuck decals on their cars that showed the U.S. flag, and other decals that said "America: Love It or Leave It!" Since then I've never hung the U.S. flag outside our house. Someone who didn't like an anti-Vietnam War letter of mine in *The Philadelphia Inquirer* sent me an unsigned postcard that began, "I am wondering if scum like you would ever have had the courage to serve in the Army." Well, in fact I had.

IT'S TRUE, THE THIRD of a century during which I taught at Penn held fewer exciting changes than the third that went before it. I helped to raise our children, rode the train to work, taught, committeed, did research, and wrote. My son-in-law, John Lally, told me once how fortunate I was to look forward to going to work each day.

Seven times we broke the even flow of years with trips to Italy. I did research in Venice, and twice I taught American (yes, American) history at the University of Perugia as a Fulbright professor, teaching in Italian. Another year I ran a study-abroad program in Bologna, a pleasant city tourists seldom see that's famous for its waistline-stretching food. I discovered in Bologna that I'd rather not become involved in students' private problems, meaning drugs, hygiene, boy friends, girl friends, arguments, theft, homesickness, and family problems in America.

Bologna students and director

It happened that in that year the University of Bologna, where our students took their courses, celebrated its 900th year. By contrast, the University of Pennsylvania pretends to have been founded in 1740.

DIFFERENT PENN PROFESSORS saw their jobs in different ways, and some would skimp on teaching. A well-known colleague told me that he always did his research in the morning, when his mind was fresh, and his teaching later in the day, when it lagged. But I found I couldn't mix my teaching and research. From September into May I spent my time entirely on teaching and committees. And playing squash.

At Penn we only spent six hours a week in class. That lightweight "load" might shock a person who doesn't know how higher education works. (Joke: State legislator to professor at state university: "How many hours do you teach?" Professor: "Nine." Legislator: "Well, that's a good day's work.")

In my office (at left is a print of Titian's portrait of Gritti)

At first I offered courses only in my "field," which was European history between the end of the Middle Ages and the French Revolution, or roughly from 1500 to 1800. When I taught the first half of Penn's survey course in European history I didn't tell my students that in a similar course at Princeton I had earned grades equivalent to B– and C.

During the 1960s, when everybody questioned everything, I was bitten by the bug of "relevance." I began to think that I should teach about events that really shaped our lives. For instance, I found it hard to justify a lecture on the Thirty Years War, which devastated Europe between 1618 and 1648. I was pretty sure that ghastly war no longer matters, isn't "relevant."

I sometimes gave a course on the history of "Wealth and Poverty." Now *that's* a topic that is relevant and something I would later write two books about. I also introduced a course on Philadelphia history, and why *not*? Philadelphia's where we *were*, my students and I. For several years I gave a course on the "Control of Life," by which I meant mankind's growing ability to prolong our lives by fighting disease and raising more to eat, while also limiting our numbers by the use of birth control.

Even when I taught about a more traditional subject, the Italian Renaissance, I wanted to be relevant. Here is an example of the problems that I faced. I used to have my students read *The Prince*, by Machiavelli, a famous little Renaissance book that illuminates how nations grew. But, I asked myself, shouldn't I be teaching more about the history of women? So should I drop *The Prince* and add to my reading list Judith Brown's *Immodest Acts: Life of a Lesbian Nun in Renaissance Italy*? Well, I compromised and had my students read both books.

As a teacher, I was fairly good, not great. I lectured, and the students and I discussed the readings which I had chosen precisely because they were interesting. But I also enriched my courses, just as you enrich a garden when you spread some compost. I played some music, took my students on field trips in Philadelphia, showed them "slides" of paintings, and took them to museums. I would have them do a "reading" of a play in class. I often took them to the Penn library's rare book room, where they could view and even gently handle medieval Bibles, written on parchment with quill pens plucked from wings of swans; a page from the first printed book, Gutenberg's Bible; and navigators' charts of European ports—things like that.

Students seemed to like my courses, but I never taught great numbers. On their course evaluation forms they sometimes called me "nice," or even "good," but never "thrilling."

Would someone tell me why the students I remember best are girls (young women), especially the pretty ones? In one of my courses in the early 1960s a pretty girl with her hair always held back by a ribbon sat in the second row. During lectures she would smile at the right moments. Fifteen years later we saw each other in a cafeteria at Penn, and she said, "You won't recall my name." I said, "You're Emily."

I remember one girl not because she was pretty but because of a paper, or the lack of one. At the end of a class, after I had handed back their papers and the other students had left, she remained. Before she spoke I said to her, "I'm embarrassed. I cannot find your paper. I must have lost it and I cannot ask you to write another. Would you accept the same grade for this one that I gave you on your earlier paper: B+?" She said, "Uh . . . Yes!" Only later did the truth occur to me.

Once in Venice I heard a young woman ask a vendor, in English, where she could buy cigarettes. I said, "I'll show you," and she startled me by saying very calmly, "Thank you, Dr. Davis." It turned out she had taken a lecture course with me at Penn, three thousand miles away. She must have thought that in the summers Penn assigned its professors to the busy spots in Europe to serve its student tourists as their guides.

THIS IS WHAT I sometimes told my students about the reasons why we study history:

MANIA

Example: Civil War buffs who want to know what every soldier did at every moment in a battle.

PREDICTION

"One who doesn't know the past is certain to repeat it. If Hitler had known what happened to Napoleon in 1812, he would have not have invaded Russia in 1941." In fact, Hitler *did* know about Napoleon. *Mad Magazine* once pointed out that "History repeats itself mainly when you flunk it."

PERSPECTIVE

This is the reason for studying history that I believe in. If you want to understand the world, it helps to know how things got where they are. Then you're not disoriented, like one who wakes in darkness. You discover who and where you are.

So what do students truly gain from study of the past? Of course I like to think they learn perspective, but I sometimes wondered *what* was sticking to their minds. Every teacher has a treasure-chest of student bloopers, and here are three of mine:

To escape, the Athenians took refuse on their ships.

Jesus said to Peter, on the Rock in Rome you will build your church.

Allegiance to the Pope was necessary for salivation.

For professors, it's prestigious to teach graduate students, but at Pennsylvania most of our grad students specialized in recent history, so I taught very few of them. And that was just as well because, starting in the 1970s, history jobs were hard to find, and most of the jobs there were now went to women or to blacks. That was fine for them but not so good for white male students who had spent a half a decade earning their advanced degrees.

Of the graduate students whose dissertations I guided, almost none went on to teach. One became a university librarian and bibliographer. Another became a minister, lived on air and prayer, and miraculously put his many children through college. Another, despite the odds, did land a teaching post and wrote two books. But then he turned into a consultant in applied microeconomics, and ended up as president and then chairman of his firm.

Even though I only taught a handful of graduate students, I served for three years as my department's graduate chairman. I used to make a point of telling our graduate students that Penn had rejected my own application for admission.

Once I served as acting chair of my department. The regular chairman had asked me to replace him while he went on leave. After I'd agreed he told me, "You will hate this job!" He gave me three good pieces of advice:

1. "Stroke" (soothe and please) our colleagues.
2. Serve beer and pizza at department meetings.
3. Make no change unless the department has voted its approval.

I did as he advised and made it through the year.

ONLY IN THE SUMMERS and on leaves did I carry out research, although, when it came to prestige and promotion, research mattered a great deal more than teaching. That research should count for more than teaching infuriates a lot of people, but that's the way it is at many universities and some colleges.

At these places a professor's job is writing articles and books that *add* to what we know. It's research, not teaching, that a university pays you for, and that's the way it ought to be. People say professors have to "publish or perish," and that sounds grim. But, speaking only for myself, I was fortunate and liked research.

Yes, professors in small colleges can mainly teach, as did my colleagues at Oberlin, and in that way make a major contribution to other peoples' lives. I have great respect for that. And they may also do research of value. But professors in a university have almost unique access to the things one needs to do research: laboratories, many, many shelves of books, research grants, and help from other scholars. A university rightly asks that they take advantage of these assets, and produce results.

Apparently my predecessor at Penn, the man who taught my "field" and then made room for me by dying, didn't know that research (and thereby adding to human knowledge) came first. In his first two decades he published almost nothing and was therefore not promoted. According to the story I was told when I arrived at Penn, he finally wrote a textbook, a task that does indeed take lots of time but not original research. Then he went to the department chairman and showed him what he'd written. "But Arthur," said the chairman, "textbooks do not count!"

Not everybody thinks that scholars' research shows their knowledge and fills a need. Someone wrote:

> We once knew a silly pants presser
> Whose knowledge grew lesser and lesser.
> It at last grew so small
> He knew nothing at all
> And now he's a college professor.

Well, what about it, you may ask, does this research that you say professors ought to do produce results that anybody *needs*? Well let's consider research in history. While I taught at Penn my History colleagues studied topics such as these: how atheism first arose in Europe, how slavery began in the New World, which groups in Germany brought Hitler to power, Japanese national culture on the eve of the attack on Pearl Harbor in 1941, and why the great powers didn't actually fight each other in the Cold War.[2] Important stuff, I'd say.

So what was Davis up to? My first important research task at Penn was publishing my dissertation on *The Decline of the Venetian Nobility as a Ruling Class*. When I had finished writing it at Hopkins I had entered it in a national competition for the year's "best unpublished manuscript" in the field of Italian history. And it won the prize, a handsome $200.00! (It's true, I later learned that no one else had entered the competition.)

Perhaps because it won this prize, the Johns Hopkins University Press published my dissertation in 1962, with an engraving of Venetian nobles on the cover. A well-known French historian, Fernand Braudel, wrote a favorable review for *The American Historical Review*. He wrote his review in French and the AHR *published* it in French, a rare event.

Venetian nobles outside the Doges' Palace

The good reception of my book may have persuaded Penn to promote me to associate professor with tenure. Tenure is important, and perhaps you are aware of this: Once they've given you tenure they cannot fire you unless you do something so unspeakable that no one knows exactly what it is.

In the meantime I had started work on two other books. One of them concerned a Venetian family, and I'll say more about it in the chapter after this.

The second book, *Pursuit of Power*, consisted of dispatches and reports written in the 1500s by ambassadors from Venice to Turkey, Spain, and France, translated into English. At first I selected the reports and another man translated them from old-fashioned Italian into English. However, when I looked at his translation I found that he had done a wretched job. For example, he thought the Italian word *viscere*, which means bowels (viscera), means viceroy. As a result he translated a phrase that really meant "dig into the bowels of the earth" as "they sent the viceroy to get it." I threw away his work and re-translated all he'd done.

To illustrate the nature of *Pursuit of Power*, here is part of a dispatch I used, printed in italics to tell the reader that the Venetian ambassador (who was living in Spain and writing to Venice) wrote it in a cipher. He tells the Venetians what the king of Spain, Philip II, may have been thinking in 1588 when he sent a fleet, the famed Armada, to fight the English:

> The wiser wonder what can induce the king to insist . . . that the Armada shall give battle to the English, who are known to be awaiting the attack with eager courage, and so they surmise that, over and above the belief that God will be on his side, two motives urge the king to this course: first that he has some secret understandings which will fail if there is any delay; secondly, that these

expenses of a million a month cannot be supported for long, and so he has resolved to try his fortune. . . .

And so he did, to his sorrow.

I found a lot of good illustrations and Harper & Row (now HarperCollins) published *Pursuit of Power* in 1970.[3] The book jacket picture, reproduced below, is an engraving that shows the killing of a French nobleman on a battlefield in 1569.

As I said above, a scholar's job is adding to our knowledge. Did my book of shortened and translated reports accomplish that? I think it did. I had made available in English documents that other historians had often heard of but were hard to find and hard to use.

MEANWHILE, I OFTEN was involved with decisions regarding tenure or promotion for other Penn professors. I served on the Arts and Sciences Personnel Committee several times and

*Death of
a French
Protestant
leader*

late in my career I chaired it once. Most colleges and universities have such committees, which usually consist of "full" professors from many departments. This is what we did: When a department recommended the promotion of an assistant or associate professor the task of our committee was to read that person's writings and the letters written about her/him by scholars in other places, and to vote. If we voted no (do not promote) custom forbade the dean's recommending the promotion to a university-wide committee that advised the provost on these matters.

And we often voted no. Here is what sometimes happened when we did. (This is only *my* opinion.) A department had voted in favor of promoting a colleague not on merit but simply because they didn't want to face this colleague, who was probably also their friend, if they voted no. In effect, they were counting on the Personnel Committee to reverse their vote of yes. However, when the committee did exactly that they shrieked in feigned indignation. How, they asked, could we, professors from other fields of knowledge, claim to be better judges of the person's merit than they, who were professors in his/her own department?

They shrieked the loudest when the candidate had earlier won a prize for excellence in teaching. Did teaching count for *nothing*?

FIVE

Lives of Rich and Poor

IT'S NOT SURPRISING that what engaged me most as an historian was wealth and poverty. In school and college I had been aware of other peoples' wealth, and that awareness has continued all my life.

When I was young, people held their ideologies solemnly. Today they don't but, just to be clear, let me mention that despite my interest in wealth and poverty I'm not a Marxist. Much of what I know of Marxism comes from having read *The Communist Manifesto* as a college student. That was sixty years ago, and even then the famous pamphlet was exactly a century old. I can understand how some of his disciples went for Marx's hazy brand of socialism, but not how others, later on, could go along with Russia's and China's Red-or-Dead variety.

Of course, we're all aware that how we live and earn our livings matters. But that's not Marx; it's common sense.

I'VE MENTIONED HOW I wrote my dissertation at Johns Hopkins about the men who ran the city-state of Venice. In my early years as a professor at the University of Pennsylvania I followed up on that research by studying the doings not of Venetian nobles in general but of one family in particular, the Donà dalle Rose. (Do not believe the folks who say I've got it wrong and the *dalle* should be *delle*. Tell them to look the name up in the Venice phone book.)

Even today members of the Donà family are living in the massive, tawny palace that Doge Leonardo Donà built in the early 1600s. This mansion stands where tourists seldom go: the side of Venice facing toward the cemetery island. At the time I wrote about the Donà, they also owned a mansion in Milan, a castle in Pavia, a villa in the foothills of the Alps, and an apartment on the island of Sardinia.

The Donà had saved two wardrobes full of family papers dating back 400 years, and Count Lorenzo Donà was glad to have me work with these. For weeks I sat on an ancient worm-gnawed armchair in his study searching through old letters, diaries, ledgers, blueprints, notes, and contracts. I never knew what I would find, and that was half the fun.

I also did research in churches, scanning ancient registers of Donà weddings, baptisms, and funerals. Once I did this in a nearly empty room where the only place that I could lay my coat was on a large glass box that held the robed and shriveled body of a priest.

From all of that research a skinny book emerged to which I gave a portly name: *A Venetian Family and Its Fortune: The Donà and the Conservation of Their Wealth.*[1] It dealt with how Venetian nobles earned the wealth that brought them power and prestige, and, more importantly, with how they managed to keep that wealth.

The point is this: Their wealth might easily have been divided and thereby lost because the Donà and other Venetian nobles married young and had great flocks of children. Here is an example: Bortolo Donà and his wife had 14 sons and daughters born in (note how short the intervals are) 1660, 1661, 1662, 1664, 1665, 1665 (again), 1667, 1668, 1669, 1670, 1672, 1673, 1675, and 1676. These nobles had to have a lot of children because so many of their brood would die and also because daughters, at that time and in that culture, didn't count. What they needed was male children, and if they had produced fewer of them the family would have risked extinction.

So here is what upper class Venetian families did in order not to let their wealth be scattered among their many children: They permitted only one of their sons to marry and thereby have heirs. A brother who didn't marry sometimes kept a mistress or he frequented the city's more expensive prostitutes. Here is one example. In the early 1500s Nicolò Donà, a bachelor, "had to do with a prostitute." (So he wrote in his will, decades later.) "I was told that she had conceived a son by me. My mother and father wanted me to acknowledge him and so I did. But he turned out worthless, conceited, and a spendthrift."

Unlike wealthy families in other places, who often passed their wealth on to their oldest sons, the rich Venetians who married and had children left their wealth to all of their legitimate sons, whether married or not, in equal shares. Apparently they did this because all their sons, as businessmen, needed money to make investments. Frequently, the sons did business as a unit, sharing what they earned. Not to leave them all a share of the estate might have destroyed the family as a business firm.

What made this seemingly risky practice of dividing the estate turn out all right was that sons who did not marry always left their shares of the estate to their nephews, the sons of the one brother in the family who had married. But suppose the only son who married had no children? Only in that case would another brother, perhaps by now in his fifties, marry in order to carry on the family.

And what about their daughters and the dowries these girls would have to pay their husbands' families if they married? In order to avoid losing money by providing marriage dow-

Villa of the Donà near Venice, now vanished

ries, parents married off as few of their daughters as possible. At a lower cost by far they put the girls who didn't marry into convents, as nuns.

The Donà I studied had many children until the 1700s when they, and other wealthy families in Venice and in other places too, began to have fewer children. Only then did birth control became another way of hanging on to wealth.

The main point that I made in this book is that families like the Donà succeeded in staying rich and powerful because they all—fathers, mothers, sons, and daughters—were willing to sacrifice their own futures for their families.

The book earned decent reviews, with one exception. A professor at a university in California wrote a review that was unpleasant and misleading, the only one I ever had. Meanwhile, I sent a copy of the book to Fernand Braudel, the French historian who earlier had given my *Decline of the Venetian Nobility* a nice review. He wrote me that this one read like a novel, "which for me is a great compliment."

Count Lorenzo Donà, the man who let me study his family's papers, was a genial old man (younger than my present age), and at the time I knew him he was having a family tomb built on Venice's cemetery island, not far across the lagoon from his palace. After breakfast every morning he would step out on his balcony with binoculars and check the workmen's progress on the tomb.

Without intending to, he taught me a lesson about the doubts we ought to have about painting attributions. Among the portraits in his palace was one of England's King James I. The count told me, and more than once I heard him telling others, that one of his ancestors had been Venice's ambassador to James's court, and that the portrait was by a "famous Flemish painter." (I think he'd say the painter's name but today I can't recall it—possibly Van Dyck.)

One day, while I was hunting through a ledger kept in the early 1600s by that ambassador's brother, I came across a note about this painting. The brother, living in Venice, wrote that he had a paid a certain minor local painter to do a portrait of King James of England because his brother had been an ambassador to that country. So here was solid evidence about who really painted the portrait of the king. I showed this ledger entry to the count, who showed great interest and had it photocopied. Not long after that, however, when he was showing guests the palace I heard him say, "This portrait is by the famous Flemish painter . . ."

WHILE I WAS WRITING about the wealth of one family and, later (as you'll see below), the poverty of another, one of my hobbies was exploring the history of my own family. What

I learned about their lives enriched my scholarly research. It also nicely illustrates the social history of American WASPs.

In earlier decades various aunts and uncles had learned about our ancestors the older way, consulting wills and hunting gravestones, and they'd written out a family tree. So when my brother Bill and I began researching we had lots of forebears' names to start from. Bill has specialized; he mostly hunts in Ireland, searching for the ancestors of our father's father. Unlike Bill I did my searching mainly on the Net, and I went back farther, adding many, many names to those that others had already found. Later, using the Net as well as published family histories, my aunts' and uncles' notes, and every will or letter I could find, I also wrote brief sketches of the lives of many forebears.

These people all had come from what we might name WASPia, a swath of northwest Europe stretching from the British Isles across the Netherlands and Germany to Sweden. Many of these immigrants, I'm sure, were younger sons of farmers who were destined not to have a portion of their families' farms, and therefore left their homes. But the immigrants also included a soldier, weaver, tailor, servant, shoe-repairman, tavern keeper, business agent, and others.

Most likely the families of these immigrants to America had been Catholics not so long before and had turned Protestant between 1500 and 1650, during Europe's religious Reformation. They had changed from WASCs to WASPs. The English ones often became Anglicans, "Puritans," Congregationalists, and sometimes Quakers, and those in Germany became Lutherans, Mennonites, and Dunkers.

The most prominent of these converts was Edwin Sandys, an Englishman who was born a Catholic but became an Anglican and in 1576/77 was made archbishop of York. He enriched his older children (I'm descended from a poorer younger one) by grabbing former Catholic Church land and adding it to the family's holdings. Once a naked woman slipped into this churchman's bed as part of a blackmail scheme. It failed.

Another English Protestant ancestor, Rebecca Cornell, was murdered in 1673 while smoking her pipe in her bedroom. One of her sons (not the one I'm descended from) was convicted of her murder and hanged. Later on, too late, a different jury found the dead man innocent of the crime. So sorry.

AT ABOUT THE TIME that most of these people became Protestants they also sailed to North America. Why? Americans like to say they came here seeking religious freedom but the forebears I'm aware of also came for land. Land was then the major form of wealth.

Through no fault of my own (as President Franklin Roosevelt once said about himself and his *Mayflower* forebears) among my American ancestors are some who came here in 1620 on the *Mayflower*. Two of them had been wool combers, one a leather tanner, one a tailor, and one a servant. But when these people got to Plymouth (Massachusetts) they mostly got along by raising crops and keeping cows.

One of these *Mayflower* ancestors who didn't farm was Isaac Allerton, the assistant to the "governor" of the tiny Plymouth colony. Allerton became a businessman and also served as agent for the colony until his fellow settlers claimed that he had cheated them in dealings with England, the home country. They said he "plaid his owne game," and exiled him. He moved not far away and ran a fishing fleet until his newer neighbors also made him leave. Meanwhile he was buying ships and trading in Virginia and the West Indies. Though storms would wreck his ships, and Indians and Frenchmen burn his trading posts, Allerton did well, even if he did not do good. He built himself a "grand house on the creek" in New Haven, Connecticut, and when he died was said to be quite rich. The problem was he owed it all to others.

In New York colony other immigrants I'm aware of did all right. By or before 1666 John Richardson and another farmer bought from local Indians a big piece of land that today is part of New York City's southeast Bronx. When they split what they had bought, Richardson took the land on the southwest side of an Indian trail that today is Hunt's Point Avenue. When Tom Wolfe wrote *The Bonfire of the Vanities* a quarter of a century ago, he set one scene in this place, which, when Wolfe wrote the book, was a terrifying slum.

Most of my ancestors worked as farmers till the nineteenth century. One example is a pioneer whose parents had given him a woman's name, Minerva. In the late 1700s Minerva Cushman married, and with his wife he moved from Connecticut to a forest in northeastern New York State, on what was then America's frontier. His son David would later write that Minerva "with another companion . . . cut their road four miles into the forest, rolled up the logs for a dwelling, covered it with bark, and cleared the land." Minerva also taught his own children and his friend's to read and write.

Meanwhile Joseph Wells, another ancestor and a son of English immigrants, purchased 90 stony acres in eastern Pennsylvania. He was 39 and his wife, Margaret, was 17. The previous owner of their land, a Scottish settler, had partially cleared it and built a cabin and small barn. The cabin consisted of a single room and an attic, where the many Wells children slept, apparently in just one bed. One of them, a son, would later write that the boards at the two ends of the attic were cracked, leaving openings "through which we often saw the moon and stars." On winter mornings the children sometimes jumped from bed "into snow an inch deep, which covered the bed and floor."

When Joseph died he left Margaret with twelve children. The son I quoted above wrote that during the fall and winter their supper was mainly mush and milk, and on one occasion the cow ran out of milk, so they all drank cider. When the cider fermented "the little ones generally went to bed in a state of partial intoxication."

Because the American colonists were always struggling against early death they did not discourage sex but tried instead to govern it. In 1645 his fellow colonists convicted Thomas Cushman, a brother of one of my Plymouth ancestors, for "committing carnal coppulation with his now wife, before marriage, but after contract." The court sentenced him to pay five pounds. A few years later a court tried my ancestor Martha Meade, a household servant, for bastardy. She testified that she was an epileptic and that she had conceived an illegitimate child during a fit and did not know who the father was. Skeptical, the court fined her ten pounds.

Until the twentieth century many children died when very young. In about 1840 my great-grandmother Mary Eliza Leggett stitched a sampler that includes a picture of a baby's coffin and these mournful lines:

> Bring flowers pale flowers o'er the bier to shed
> A crown for the brow of the living dead
> For this in the woods were the violets nursed
> For this through its leaves has the white rose burst.
> Though they smile in vain for what once was ours
> They

Maybe bored with death, she stopped her stitching after "They."

In a way those verses were prophetic. Later, Mary's older sister, who had seen several of her five children die, also died. Mary then married her brother-in-law and had five children by him.

Americanization may have been easier for the English immigrants than for my great-great-great-(take a breath)-great-great-grandfather Hendrik Pfannebecker, who was born in western Germany. He came to Pennsylvania in the late 1600s, and made his living as a farmer, miller, and surveyor. He wrote this letter in 1742, when he had been in the New World nearly fifty years:

Frind Edward Shippen

My Keind Respek too Juw too let Ju understan tha I haffe Spoken With the totters of Abraham op then graff [Op De Graff, which later became Updegrove and other variations] an by ther Words are Willing too Sings [sign] Jur deets as ther broders haffe don. Now more att this pressents as mey Keind Resspeck too Ju an Jor broder.

From Jur frind
Henry Pannebecker

As his signature reveals, even if he had kept his accent Hendrik Pfannebecker had altered his first and last names. Many of his early descendants were buried in the same eastern Pennsylvania cemetery and on their gravestones their last name was spelled five ways. Today there are 31 different spellings of the name. My mother's family spells it Pennypacker.

I had wrongly assumed that my Yankee ancestors would not have owned slaves, but historians of slavery such as my former colleague Richard Dunn have told me otherwise. One such slave owner was Gabriel Leggett, who farmed the land in New York City's south Bronx that his father-in-law John

Richardson had earlier bought from Indians. Gabriel also ran a sawmill and cut lumber, which was used in building houses in what is now the Harlem district of New York City. In his will, written in about 1698, Gabriel left to a daughter "my little Negro Boy," and when his widow later drew up her will she left to another daughter "two negro children born of the body of Hannah my negro woman, and of the issue of the body of Robin my Indian slave." Indian slaves were rare, since Indians could so easily slip off into forests. You'll notice that the widow calls the offspring of an Indian man and a "negro" woman "negro children."

It may have been Gabriel's older brother John who bought their slaves for the Leggetts since John did business in the West Indies, where slaves were sold. In his will, drawn up in 1680, John Leggett left these items to his son: his clothing; his half of a small sailing ship; barrels of sugar, rum, and lime juice (potentially the makings of many rum Collinses); and "one negro" known as "You-Boy."

BY THE LATER 1850s only one ancestor I'm aware of made his living farming. This was John Pennypacker, who ran a small dairy farm called "Garden Spot" in eastern Pennsylvania and sold his butter once a week at a farmers' market in Philadelphia. And in about 1870 even John stopped farming. He became a butcher, and his wife cooked meals for boarders.

A striking example of the shift from farming is the career of Don Alonzo Cushman. His parents, the oddly-named pioneer Minerva and his wife, had given all their first six children names that start with D: Deborah, Diodama, Delia, Diodate, Don Alonzo, and David. From his father Don Alonzo learned to read and write, and a prisoner in a village jail taught him how to keep a ledger. Then Don Alonzo left the home his father had built from logs and moved to New York City, where he made a fortune in banking and selling real estate. He married, built a mansion, traveled in Europe, enjoyed the opera, and often suffered indigestion.

John Griffen was raised on a farm just north of New York City but he left it in his teens and later ran a bridge-building company in eastern Pennsylvania. He invented a way of making wrought iron cannons, and during the Civil War the iron company he worked for produced these cannons for the North. An artilleryman said the cannon "could hit the end of a flour barrel at any distance under a mile more often than not, unless the gunner got rattled."

As THEIR INCOMES rose, and as they left their farms for towns, almost all my ancestors switched from being Congregationalists, Presbyterians, Quakers, Lutherans, Mennonites, Dunkers, or something else, to being Episcopalians. They may have looked at their conversions as a rise in social status.

Here is one intriguing switch. John Griffen, the iron-maker and cannon-inventor, and his second wife Mary were raised as Quakers, but they became Episcopalians in the 1860s. According to a family story, they made this switch after Griffen invented his cannon and a delegation from his Quaker meeting, all pacifists, came to him and told him that the meeting had expelled him.

However, an autobiographical letter that Griffen wrote a friend in 1878 tells a different tale about his family's switch from Quakers to Episcopalians. He makes no mention of the cannon, and writes that he and his family ceased to be Quakers because they enjoyed singing and playing billiards, and the local Quakers disapproved. He wrote, "they set their faces against music, and also largely against innocent games; not that they think there is any harm in the thing itself, but that it may lead to harm."[2]

The wealthy Don Alonzo Cushman had been raised on the frontier as a Presbyterian. However, by the middle 1800s, when he was prospering in New York City, he was a devout Episcopalian. He said grace before and after meals, and required all his family to attend morning family prayers, evening family prayers, and a Sunday night service at which he read a sermon.

As WE SAW, Wellses and Cushmans had lived in cabins and near-poverty in the early 1800s. By way of contrast, Gustavus William Faber and his wife (Don Alonzo Cushman's daughter) lived very well in New York City in about 1900. Gustavus was a cigar importer, whose surname can still be seen today on Faber candy and magazine stores. He and his family lived in New York City's Chelsea section in a handsome brick-and-brownstone row house that had three floors above ground and two below it.

My father, who recalled his Faber grandparents well, told me once that six maids and a "furnace man" attended to their wants. Their Christmas parties featured a tree with candles that were lighted and then promptly put out (for fear of fire); a Punch and Judy show for the children; a $20 gold piece for each child and a $5 gold piece for each grandchild; and oysters, turkey, several other courses, a pudding made from chestnuts and candied fruit, and red wine and champagne. In the summers the Fabers often rented a boarding house in Connecticut, and hosted 30 family members for two weeks. Automobiles were in their infancy, so the Fabers leased a railroad car to move the extended family from New York to Connecticut.

The income of my mother's parents, James and Fannie Pennypacker (the daughter of iron-maker John Griffen), must have been a fraction of the Fabers'. In 1900 James's salary as superintendent of an iron-rolling mill in eastern Pennsylvania was $2,000 per year. In that same year the income of the steel-maker Andrew Carnegie was $25,000,000, and he paid no income tax. So his income was roughly 13,000 times as great as James'. James' working hours were seven to twelve and one to six on weekdays, and half of that on Saturday, for a total of 55 hours.

The Pennypackers' income was tiny when compared to Carnegie's but it was higher than the U.S. average. They lived in a three-story brick twin house and always had a maid, first an Irish one, then a black who died of tuberculosis, and later still a "Slavic" one (whatever "Slavic" may have meant). Fannie also had a Hungarian cleaning woman who brought her baby boy to work, where he slept on a blanket on the Pennypackers' kitchen floor. Several decades later he would own a large automobile dealership outside the town.

My casual findings about the history of my own family were linked to my two "serious" family histories. In part they resulted from the book I had already written about the wealthy Donà family in Venice. They also taught me things that I would use in writing about another, very different family.

IT OCCURRED TO ME one summer when we were in Italy that our children ought to know a bit about the life of Elda's father, Franc (pronounced *frahnts*) Žužek. So I asked him questions about his life, never telling him the reason lest he tell me nothing more. I later wrote a sketch of his life, and published it in an historical journal.[3]

My work on Žužek family history might have ended there if I hadn't come across some splendid sources for the family's history a few years later. I visited the priest in a village near the

Žužeks' and discovered that his church (which the Žužeks had attended since its founding in about 1780) had records of weddings, births, and deaths dating back two hundred years.

I decided to explore the Žužeks' lives. Other historians— I for one—had written histories of wealthy families, but I'm pretty sure that no one had ever written more than a few pages about a poor one. (I may be wrong.) I had what may have been a unique opportunity to write about a family who, until nearly 1890, had been illiterate. Most historians wouldn't have had those church registers or the access that I had to my Žužek in-laws.

As always, the research was fun. I examined the church registers, often shocked by the high infant mortality they revealed, and I went to records offices hunting maps of plots of land, and I hunted everywhere for photographs. I interviewed a lot of Žužeks and their friends, and I talked to local historians who helped me to set the Žužeks' story in a larger context. A professor who was an expert on Slovene personal and place names helped me to avoid mistakes. (For example, *žužek* means *insect* but *Žužek* may not derive from *žužek*.)

Once I had a triumph when I found a certain Žužek's name carved on a limestone cistern in front of an ancient stone-roofed house in a nearby village. I had already figured that this house had been the family's long-time home but that carving made it nearly certain. Therefore "my" Žužeks were probably descended from a serf named Jurij (George) Žužek, who had lived in that house in the 1500s.

I could learn some things regarding Jurij from the charter of his lord, who had governed from the castle of Duino, several miles away. A copy of that charter, written in a German script that's hard to read, is in the archives of Trieste. It says that Jurij was obliged to pay certain items to the prince each year.

These payments included olive oil, which (the charter says) was burned to light the prince's chapel, firewood, three kinds of grain, vegetables, and a sum of money.

Although I could uncover a few facts about the Žužeks of earlier centuries, most of what I could learn about them began in the year 1800. In that year Tomaž (Thomas) Žužek, born in the hamlet of Slivno, married Marina Gabrovic of the hamlet of Vižovlje, about a mile away. He moved to Vižovlje and probably took over the farming of her family's land.

Vižovlje (where Elda would grow up a century later) was primitive and poor. In Tomaž's lifetime it was a cluster of 14 small, gray-stone houses-with-cowsheds that almost blended into the rocky, treeless slope they stood on. Its people (a tax official reported in 1823) were "poorly nourished, but strong, and able to bear up under the toil of the farm." Old engravings of the Carso show that the men wore tattered woolen shirts, knee breeches, and broad-brimmed hats, and the women dirndls and kerchiefs.

Tomaž grazed his few sheep and cattle in the rocky pastures and he raised some grain and vegetables on little plots of land where the violent winter wind hadn't carried off the soil. The plots and pastures were probably the same land that his descendants still were farming a century later: sixteen scattered acres which are recorded at the castle of Duino merely as pasture but some of which he may have used for crops, and twenty acres good only for firewood. During Tomaž's lifetime the Žužeks and their neighbors were still at least partially serfs, and for the right to use those 36 acres Tomaž paid his lord at Duino dues in money and perhaps in work.

Using the first-rate parish registers, I could tell my readers quite a lot about the Žužeks' lives. Marina bore 11 children, of whom no less than eight died within one year of birth.

The local priest recorded what he guessed were the causes of their early deaths: Three had died of "weakness," two of "ordinary" causes, one of "swollen throat," and two of tuberculosis or some other wasting sickness. Soon after giving birth to her last child Marina died at 36. She may have starved to death in a time of famine.

The Žužeks' poverty and early deaths continued over several generations. But ripple effects from the Industrial Revolution may have slightly eased their lives toward the end of the 1800s. Now they could supplement their incomes by hauling blocks of marble in their ox cart from the nearby quarries to the marble cutters maybe seven miles away. It was while returning from such a trip in June of 1901 that Jožef Žužek (Elda's grandfather) had a fatal heart attack or stroke. The oxen knew the way and eventually they reached the village, pulling the cart with Jožef's body lying on the hay. I like the drawing reproduced here from the Italian translation of my book about the Žužeks,[4] even though the two oxen only have six legs.

Jožef, dead, arrives in Vižovlje

Elda's father, Franc, was one of Jožef's younger sons. His oldest brother inherited the family's land, so Franc worked all his life at hauling stone, building roads, and working in a shipyard. He married a young woman who had also held a lot of jobs, including packing sardines in barrels. They had five children, the last of whom was Elda.

During World War I shells fired from the sea by Italian ships flattened Vižovlje. It was then rebuilt, but a generation later, during World War II, German soldiers burned it, gutting the houses. After the war the hamlet was rebuilt again.

I named my book about the Žužeks *Rise from Want: A Peasant Family in the Machine Age.*[5] In the preface I wrote, "Please understand that this book was written not only for those with a scholarly interest in the subject but for all those who have, somewhere among their ancestors, a poor peasant or two." I tried to make the book readable, and forgive me when I tell you that reviewers praised it highly. In the United States it only sold modestly because it deals with a place Americans have never heard of, but Italian and Slovene presses published translations, and the Italian version soon sold out, was reprinted, and sold out again.

Books can lead to odd results. I mentioned in my book that on one occasion a girl had "wandered behind the house one day and found her stepmother in a compromising attitude with a young man." This carefully worded sentence caused some problems with her stepmother's family for that witness, who (when my book appeared) was now a middle-aged woman. Angrily she said to me, "I don't know where you heard that tale."

But I knew, though I didn't say so. I had heard it from her. Anyway, she told me that if I'd cut that sentence from the Italian translation, which then was in the works, she would not be angry any more. So I left that sentence out of the Italian version, but she still was unforgiving. So when a translation into Slovene was prepared I put the sentence back in place.

WHEN AN ASSASSIN murdered Martin Luther King in 1968 I went with two professor friends to a memorial ceremony outside Philadelphia's Independence Hall. As we stood there, one of these good friends, himself an able and productive historian, said, "King was 39 and so am I. He did so much, and what have I done?"

I've sometimes asked myself that question. I know that I taught as well as I could and tried to make known what I learned about the past, especially about the lives of rich and poor.

Years later I would write these words about my career for my Hill School class's *Fiftieth Reunion Yearbook:*

> [An] oldster asked me, "What exactly did you do?" I found it hard to answer. I taught a lot of students things they didn't know they wanted to know, sat on committees that never figured out how to make students study or professors profess, and wrote books that almost no one wanted to read. I would do it all again.

SIX

Wordstruck Klutz

EARLY IN THIS BOOK I wrote about learning where I am and deciding what I wished to be. Those are problems that we face when young and only starting down the road. But now that I'm old, I'll settle for figuring out who I am and what I've seen and know. That's enough—perhaps too much—to hope for.

A psychologist, Howard Gardner, has suggested that there isn't only one kind of intelligence but about ten and that these are distributed among us unequally.[1] (And some would say unfairly, only fairness never was the deal with life.) Rating myself according to three of Gardner's categories, I think I have good "linguistic intelligence" and adequate "interpersonal intelligence" (interacting sensitively), but am only barely passing when it comes to "intrapersonal intelligence," which means understanding one's self. That may have been the reason why I later suffered from depression, which I'll write about in Chapter 7.

As everybody knows, a klutz is one who's clumsy, foolish, and inept. That is what I often am and here is one example: When I took my driver's license test at the age of 17 the test did not go well. The family Chevy had a manual transmission, and every time I started it, the car would snarl and buck before it moved. At the end, the examiner told me that I'd started it each time in third gear, not in first. He looked at me thoughtfully and said, "I'm going to pass you. I really don't know why."

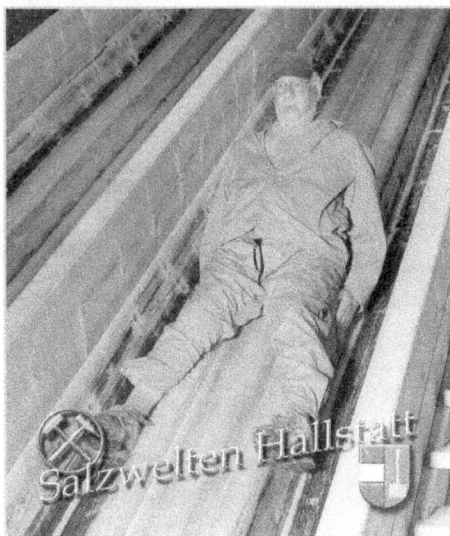

Frightened klutz in an Austrian salt mine

Believe you me, when someone says that he's a klutz, a klutz he is. I'm poor at understanding even how a simple gadget does its job. I don't know how a zipper works, and I still won't if you tell me. And I have no sense of direction, so I find my way by turning this memorized way at the crossing, and that memorized way at the light. Naturally, I easily get lost. How did I survive in Venice, that maze of cul-de-sacs?

As a one-time English major, I should at least partly understand the books I read, but I'm not quite sure I do. In 1923 the Italian writer Italo Svevo published his finest novel, *Confessions of Zeno.* Because the setting of the story is Trieste, the city where I served while in the Army, I've read the *Confessions* twice at least. In this imaginary memoir, Zeno is a young and likable—even charming—businessman. He's happily married, has some friends, and earns a decent income. However, try as he may he can't quit smoking, so he sees a psychoanalyst.

Now, here's my point. Where I see Zeno as I've pictured him above, other readers see him as neurotic. For example, the blurb on the back cover of an English translation of *Confes-*

sions calls it "the story of a doubting, guilt-ridden man. . . . As a form of therapy, his doctor advises him to write his memoirs; in doing so, Zeno . . . reshapes the events of his life into a palatable reality . . . founded upon compromise, delusion, and rationalization."

And yet I still see Zeno as basically content, not "doubting" and not torn by guilt. Perhaps I've got him wrong. I told you I'm a klutz.

I ask you this: Is orderliness a sign of cleverness or desperation? I keep a long To Do list, and every morning after breakfast I consult it to see what I must do that day. I constantly revise the list.

For the pockets of my pants I use this system: right front pocket: sales slips; left front: papers to discard; left rear: wallet; right rear: comb and keys. I'm always weeding through my clothes and papers, throwing out the stuff I'll never need. As for books, I keep as many as can fill eight shelves, and any time I add a book I throw another book away.

What do dreams reveal about my inner self? Some medical researchers believe that dreams have no significance. They say that dreams occur as our nerve cells are recovering from the labors of the day and our minds are trying to make sense of what those cells are doing. Many psychologists, on the other hand, believe that dreaming is the way our minds arrange the things we've seen and done in daytime. They're storing new information in such a way that it connects with things we know already, and they filter what has happened and identify significant events.[2]

Like most of us, I rarely do recall my dreams. However, several years ago for about a month I made an effort to remember them. As others have discovered, if I wrote my dreams down just as soon as I awoke I could remember some. I later talked to my psychiatrist (who will appear again in the next chapter) about these dreams, but he didn't show much interest. He suggests that dreams do not provide the insights that we need.

Well, that's what he says, and I value his opinion, but to me the content of many of those dreams suggests self-doubt. Here are just a few of the disturbing ones.

I'm a student and I have a bewildering first day of classes.

I'm a student, and exams are nearing and I'm unprepared. I have never gone to classes in two courses, and I'm not even sure that I'm enrolled in them.

I wander, lost, in some confusing building.

I play doubles tennis, but all four of us are duffers.

I'm in the Army, and an inspection will take place in just five minutes. Frantically I prepare.

I'm an aged student, and our young, dynamic teacher asks us questions I can't answer. He suggests I drop the course.

I'm a professor, and I teach a class badly.

I'm a professor, and at a committee meeting I ask a stupid question. The others look at me with scorn.

However, not all my dreams that month were bad. For example:

I'm in the palace of the Donà family, whom I wrote about in *A Venetian Family*. I walk through vast and splendid rooms with silk-brocaded walls I never knew were there.

And here's a dream that's even funny:

A group of us entice some bears inside a cellar. We somehow put them to sleep and I trim the claws of one unconscious bear. Then we go upstairs and ask ourselves, how *will* we get rid of those bears in the cellar?

Here's my favorite dream:

I'm on a trolley passing through three Philadelphia neighborhoods I know. Germantown is an 1800s mill town with smoking
chimneys and teams of horses pulling wagons piled with goods.
In Mount Airy, handsome buildings line the street. They extend
above it just as European houses often hung above the streets five
hundred years ago. In Chestnut Hill we drive by gorgeous palaces.
Between them we have splendid views of castles, farms, and lofty,
rounded hills.

I AM A KLUTZ but a klutz who's wordstruck, and likes to
write. I borrowed "wordstruck" from the title of the memoirs
of the journalist, Robert MacNeil. *Wordstruck* isn't in my dictionary but it ought to be.

I like to write, but it's difficult to discuss what I think about
my writing without appearing to believe I do it well. In fact, I
write better than many but not as well as hosts of others. You
have to keep in mind that most of us historian/scholars are not
aiming at a crowd. We mostly write for others in "our field" so
we seldom try to write with charm.

Writing well is hard. Theodore White, a journalist who wrote
very readable accounts of U.S. Presidential elections, mentions
somewhere in *his* memoirs having had "those bursts of ecstasy
when the hours of writing swept by like minutes, all the words
flowing in paragraphs pre-shaped by unconscious thinking."[3] I
only wish the hours and words would flow like that for me.

Instead I write in spurts. With lots of writhing, many pauses,
gazing out the window, looking at my watch, checking my To
Do list, and visiting the fridge, I write perhaps a hundred words.
Only *then* begins the part I like: the tinkering and tuning up.
Now I make a thousand changes in those hundred words. I try
to make the point I'm making clear, of course, and to obey the
writer's Golden Rule: If in doubt leave it out.

Next day I read again the words I just described. I throw away a half, tinker with the rest, CUT some out, PASTE some back, and move some somewhere else. And that's the way my book takes shape: two steps forward, one step back, and two steps to the side.

In painting pictures I'm the same. I'm at best a dauber; you can take my word for that. But my painting method is the same one that I use when writing: always touching up. I used to paint with watercolors but it's true what people say: With them you can't make errors. No tinkering allowed, no scores of tiny changes that will only muddy the result. So now I've switched and use acrylic paints; they quickly dry and let you paint right over what you did. Now I paint in just the fussy way I write.

Compared to a former colleague at the University of Pennsylvania, I'm a slow and lazy writer. Paul Fussell taught in Penn's English Department while I was teaching history, and believe it or not, we never met. That tells a little about Penn and a lot about me. But anyway I know the way he writes because, like me, he wrote his memoirs and, like me, he writes about the way he writes. Fussell says that during the two-thirds of the year when he was teaching, he also did research. (That's a two-at-oncer I could never do.) Then he did his writing in the summer, drafting half a dozen pages every day. In just one summer he produced a book "after one writing and one rewriting."[4] Only one!

Here's a writing matter that is technical but, to me, important. I sometimes write in iambs, which typically are used in poems but not in prose. An iamb is a rhythm unit made up of an unstressed syllable followed by a stressed one. Like: Ta TUM. I used them just above: "are USED in POEMS but NOT in PROSE." I write in iambs only when I try to and the thing I want to say permits.

You might suppose that at the University of Pennsylvania, where two bright men invented the computer in 1946, all professors immediately started using those machines that very year. Not so. Most professors, like people everywhere, didn't have computers until decades later.[5] Till then I wrote on portable typewriters: first a battered American Remington; then an elegant Italian Olivetti; then a sturdy German Olympia.

But then one day I watched a secretary at Penn using a computer for word-processing. (Secretaries got computers well before professors.) To a man who typed so slowly, seeking out each key and often hitting one beside it, it was splendid how she quickly made corrections, shaped a footnote, or transposed some words. She could swiftly copy what she typed and store the copy elsewhere, thus avoiding missing-manuscript disasters that destroy careers.

By the early 1980s computers were small enough to lift without a crane, so Penn began to buy them for professors. When I first received a Mac I was in my fifties, an age when people don't adapt as quickly as before. But I loved it from the start and in the prefaces of my books I always thank dear "Mia Macintosh." I love the little devil even when she gives me problems. (I should wear one of those T-shirts that say, "SMASH FOREHEAD ON KEYBOARD TO CONTINUE.")

I DO LOVE WORDS, but not the mindless blah that no one needs. Once I wrote a TV station that their weather people shouldn't say "precipitation in the form of rain" when all they meant was "rain." No one wrote me back. Once when I was bothered by conversation stuffers (such as *like* and *you know*) I wrote this limerick:

A ditsy young airhead named Bruno
Went swimming with walri near Juneau.
He shivered and shook,

This ice-covered schnook,
And stammered "l-like!" and "y-you know!"

Names are fun. Once I wrote a letter to *The Philadelphia Inquirer* about the names of local teams (the "Flyers,""Eagles," and the "Seventy-Sixers"). I suggested that the names should be not goody-goody but city-gritty. I suggested "Pit Bulls," "Roaches," or "Addytoods." They didn't print my letter.

Once I wrote my fellow History professors at Penn an official-looking letter giving a "revised list" of interdisciplinary committees on which (I said) the colleagues whom I named would serve. They included:

Verbal expression	Hackney, Kors
Aging process	Childers, Faust
Abnormal psychology	Kuklick, Lewin
Male sexuality	Peters, Dwork

Can you stand another? When I wrote the preface to my history of Elda's family, *Rise from Want,* I thanked "the authors cited . . . from Adamcek to Zinsser, from Nice to Nasti, from Prude to Gross." Those surnames really were in the bibliography.

Speaking of names, I've often lived in places that had cheerful ones suggesting beauty. I was born on Fairview Avenue and I went to college in the "Garden State" (New Jersey). I had basic training at Fort Belvoir (another "beautiful view") in Virginia, and in the Army in Italy I lived for a while in the Bella Vista (yet another "beautiful view") Hotel. Our oldest son was born in a Pennsylvania town called Bellefonte, which means "beautiful spring" of water. I taught for a year in a state whose official song is "Beautiful Ohio," and when I was a Fulbright professor we lived in Florence on Via di Bellosguardo (yet *another* "beautiful view").

WHEN IT COMES to English-language spelling reform I'm something of a nut, and here's the point: As our world has shrunk, humans everywhere have interlinked. These links have pushed the spread of English to the point where those who speak it as a first or second language number more than half a billion, roughly eight percent of all the people on the Earth. This spreading of our language may be fine for those of us who grew up speaking English, since if they will speak like us we needn't learn to speak like them. But think about the task that billions yet unborn in other lands will face in learning English! The grammar's easy but the spelling is insane! Imagine how much time they'll waste in learning how to spell and say such words as *rough* and *foreign*.

I have sometimes pointed to this global problem in our Davis family Season's Greetings letters. For example:

> A comitee of reformrs hav sujestd spelng chanjes that make sens. They cal ther systm "Cut Spelng." Be practicl, they say. Dont thro out our presnt "systm," simplify. And y not? Lets be kind to thos in othr lands ho hav to lern our wel belovd, crazi mothr tong. Th main thing is omitng th unecesary letrs. Many of thes redundntces ar obvius.
>
> Wel, enuf on spelng. U don't want to read another wrd about it and u shant.

Although these memoirs deal with me, I can't leave out the woman I've been married to for nearly 55 years, nor our children. These are excerpts from our annual "season's greetings" letters:

> [1970] Elda sews, knits, embroiders, cooks, cans, freezes, nurses ailing children, and routs invading dogs from morn to night.

> [1980] She is very much concerned with vegetables: growing them and worrying about whether her little children (aged 25, 23, and 20) eat enough of them.

[1994] Last spring Elda became a U.S. citizen. [For 40 years she had refused to do so.] In her exam she correctly answered all the political/historical questions. But she says she still is not American.

[1995] Elda was shopping, and she pushed her cart to the end of the checkout line. A woman who was already there said, "I was here first," and Elda said, "No problem." It turned out that they come from villages in Italy that are only 50 miles apart. Rina and Elda became close friends.

[2005] While Elda was planting daisies by our curb, a driver stopped his bus, opened the door, and called to her, "We're awarding you an A plus for your garden." As he drove away his passengers all waved.

Elda watches money with a miser's care. Many years ago she and our three children and I had dinner in a small Italian restaurant. When we asked the owner/waitress for the check she brought us one that only said "10,000 lire." Clearly, she had simply multiplied a standard price (2,000) by the five of us. Elda then demanded that the check be itemized, so the woman went away and returned with one that totaled *more:* 10,300. When Elda protested at this increase, the woman said, "Signora, if you'll simply pay 10,000, that will be just fine." So we did.

Elda runs a plant sale every year in May, selling hundreds of perennials she has dug up from her gardens all around our house. For her, the fun is in the dealings with the clients, lots of whom return each year. We advertise this event in our local weekly paper: "Pretty good plant sale. You could do worse!"

Our children appeared between 1955 and 1960. I sometimes wonder, how did they grow up while I was busy having my career at Penn? The answer is that Elda did the most part of the raising.

(L. to r.) Jim, Miriam, Elda, Daniel, David

However, while the children still were small I had the task of putting David and Daniel to bed and reading to them. We read a lot of splendid yarns: *The Yearling, Treasure Island, Kim, Tom Sawyer*, and, of course, John Masefield's well-named tale about an English boy's adventures, *Jim Davis.*

At times our children caused us worry. The two boys used to hunt for snakes in nearby woods, and once they disappeared for hours. Hysterically Elda and I asked each other whether a peculiar bachelor neighbor known as "Mr. Bag" had seized them in the woods. We raised a neighborhood alarm, and searched for blocks around our house. We didn't find the boys and drove back home quite scared. When we got there, whom did we see but Mr. Bag himself, standing on the sidewalk in front of our house. In his shy and awkward way he said, "They're home."

When Miriam was in her early teens, her best friend's father drove the two girls to a Philadelphia hotel. As we understood it, a convention of beauticians was meeting there, and a demonstrator would give the two girls permanent waves. When the girls did not come home on time I phoned the hotel, and whoever answered told me no convention was occurring there! We jumped to frightening conclusions. But it was all a mix-up, and soon the girls came home, well permed.

As children always do, our three evolved as different adolescents. David was bright and serious, but with a sense of humor. Daniel was a perfectionist, a maker of friends and runner of risks. Miriam was fun, orderly, and a favorite of her teachers. The three of them grew up, married splendid spouses (Susan, Yvonne, and John) and produced five over-average children: Nathan, Kevin, Lauren, and Kristen. The 'ns. Plus Leah.

In 2004 Elda and I celebrated our 50th wedding anniversary, and our children and our grandkids threw a splendid party. The printed invitations to this bash contained a photograph that was taken at our wedding 50 years before. It showed a loving wedding pair. Stirred by this, my cousin Barbara Worcester, who couldn't come to the party, emailed us these limericks:

> If I hadn't been asked I might madden,
> But the fact I can't come makes me sadden.
> Just to look at the joy
> Of that young girl and boy
> Turns the sadden, not madden, to gladden.

> Let's drink to the beautiful life
> Fifty years brought this hist prof and wife.
> Let's toot tantaRAs
> And beat noisy huzZAHs
> On historically *echt* drum and fife!

(*Echt* is German for "correct." Barbara went to Bryn Mawr.)

HERE IS AN EXAMPLE of the way my travels stretched my views. Once I flew to India, my expenses partly paid by a society that promotes knowledge of India. These excerpts from my travel diary show my interest in the way the people lived:

> Arrived Bombay [now Mumbai] airport. Taxi ride to hotel w/Sikh driver. . . . Slums immediately apparent—small clusters of huts on vacant lots.

> [Mumbai] Taj Mahal Hotel. Elegant bellboys, reception desk staffed by pretty women. . . . Lobby of hotel cosmopolitan in extreme. Every dress. Arabs, Chinese, Africans, Indians, Americans.

> [Mumbai] At traffic light my taxi driver nearly hits foot of young man on motorcycle with girl in sari. [Young man asks in English] "Is that your sense of justice, to run over my foot?" Later driver returns me to hotel, driving through prostitution district. Driver says 10,000 women there.

> [Madras] [My guide] says Russian tourists smell of bad perfume and are utterly uninterested in Hinduism and its art. Germans are informed and thorough. The Italians and the French want once-over lightly. Americans want to know where bathrooms are.

> [Madras] My guide and I visit a village. People friendly, send small boy up high palm for coconuts for guide and me. Guide says village people always hospitable like this. Thirty people walk back to car with us, bringing coconut for driver. I ask guide, does the village have "untouchables"? She says yes, but they would live apart and keep their distance.

> [New Delhi] Guide tells me Hindu values have nothing to do with high number of children. Families have children (and want sons) for economic security in old age, and, in former times, to defend family in vendettas with other families. Guide tells me of conversation with poor and ignorant Hindu in old Delhi. Man considering vasectomy but told by others it would make him sexually impotent and also too weak to do his daily physical work. Crowd of workmen gathered, listening. My guide told them he

had been vasectomized years ago with none of those effects and they should do it for themselves and India.

[Near Kajuraho temples] Large field just below [hotel] window is planted with grain. All afternoon two women, one in bright red sari and other in blue one, patrolled it, monotonously shouting "Hey!" at the birds that threatened to eat the seedlings, and swinging stones in slings. Meanwhile a cow repeatedly slipped through a hedge into a large garden in front of the hotel, and ate some grass and flowers. Gardeners must have chased her away at least 10 times.

[Varanasi] In the filthy streets I saw two young American men dressed in the clothing style of [Indian] holy men, incredibly dirty and barefoot [as if they were mocking India's poverty].

I USED TO BE quite unaware that the place of women in the home or workplace wasn't as it should be. One reason for my ignorance may have been that I grew up mostly in the company of males. I had no sisters, and in those years from the '30s to the '50s there were no girls at Camp Awosting, Hill School, Princeton, or the Army. At Hopkins a few of my fellow graduate students were women, but it happens that I didn't know them well. In Oberlin's history department all of us professors were men.

In the year that I was hired by Penn, 1960, professors from another university interviewed me for a job at the "slave market," the annual meeting of the American Historical Association. While they were talking to me in a hotel room, a young woman who also had an appointment with them poked her head inside the door. She asked them, "Is it worth my time to wait? Would you hire a woman?" Yes, they said, of course we would. In a week or two they wrote and offered me the job, so I went to their university to see what it was like. While chatting with a young professor there who had been present at my interview I asked him if it was true that they would have hired a woman. He told me, "never."

Instead of going to that university, I took the job at Penn, where—no great surprise—the History Department had no female professors. At that time, those against the hiring of a woman used to argue that she would only marry, raise a family, and do no research. I must confess, I half believed that that was true. However, in the 1960s we at Penn began to hire women. Among them was my friend Lynn Lees, who since her hiring has raised two children (with her husband's help of course), written books, and for six years chaired the History Department.

In the early 1960s my alma mater Princeton first considered admitting undergraduate women students, but some alumni threatened that if it did this they would never give another cent to the university. So I wrote a letter to the *Princeton Alumni Weekly* pushing for this change. Penn was coed, and modestly I offered my opinion that coeducation works.

Meanwhile America has been diversifying, not only in gender but also in race or ethnicity, as anyone who walks down city streets will know. Not only are others joining us, especially from Asia and Latin America, but some who have long been living near us now are really, truly joining us. We are, as people say, "transitioning." It used to be that WASPs (or WMASPs, White *Male* Anglo-Saxon Protestants) were in control but now that's coming to an end. We're going to be a nation run by all.

In all the places where I grew up and started my career, blacks were few. In our New Jersey town the nearest blacks (then "colored") resided in "the Valley," several blocks away, but no black children went to nearby public schools. As with women, no blacks went to Hill School, and none were in my class at Princeton. A few blacks were in my Army basic train-

WASPs at David's wedding

ing company in Virginia but, supposedly because of an agree-
ment between Italy and America, none at all were stationed
in Trieste. I can't recall a single black in grad school at Johns
Hopkins, and until the later 1960s no blacks taught in Penn's
history department.

I do wish I could say that in my school and college years I
waved my arms and screamed about de facto segregation. The
truth is that I rarely gave the problem any thought. Well yes,
it's true that as a reporter on the *Daily Princetonian* I wrote
a feature story on Paul Robeson's boyhood. Robeson was a
famous black actor and singer—you can hear his deep, appeal-
ing voice for free on YouTube—who had grown up in the town
of Princeton's "colored" neighborhood. I interviewed some people there who had known him, and I wrote to Robeson, but he
didn't answer. So I quoted from a speech in which he'd said
that Princeton blacks "lived for all intents and purposes on a
Southern plantation."

It was someone else's protest though that really woke me up. This happened later, when I was a graduate student at Johns Hopkins. In a men's room in our building there were three toilet stalls, and on one of them was stenciled, in big letters, the word JANITOR. Another graduate student (white) made an issue of this, saying "JANITOR" meant "NEGRO" or "COLORED." The outcome was that someone painted out the offensive word. I too had seen it, but until the other student's protest I hadn't *really* seen it.

Later, in a letter to a Philadelphia paper in my early years at Penn I pointed out that (as was usual) not a single black took part in that year's Mummers parade. (This annual New Year's Day parade of Philadelphia amateur clowns and string bands is an old tradition.) I signed my name and under it I typed "History, Penn." I soon received a letter from a woman who protested my "disgusting letter." She wrote that she "surmised you are either black or a low-down do-gooder." A man who claimed to be a Penn alumnus wrote to me that what I said was "unthinkable" and that I should stick to teaching "History if you can and not afro under any consideration. On second thought you must be stupid."

IN AMERICA THE DIVISION between whites and blacks is partly based on backgrounds, things that some groups know and others don't. In about 1970 I served on a jury in Philadelphia in the trial of a black woman accused of shooting to death her husband's "girl friend." The murder had occurred in North Philadelphia, where many blacks reside. Just before the shooting, the woman on trial had been in an apartment on the second floor of the house in front of which the murder had occurred.

My point involves that second-floor apartment. When we, the jury, deliberated, it came out that the eight black members of the jury had understood what the four white ones hadn't: The apartment was a "speak," an illegal bar whose owner sold untaxed whiskey. Since it was testified that the murder victim had been very drunk, the nature of that apartment mattered.

If you're curious, we acquitted the accused.

Here is a revealing moment I observed in 1995. After months of hearings a jury was about to give its verdict in the murder trial of a well-known black football player and sports pundit, O. J. Simpson. Maybe 20 staffers, other professors, and I were standing at the bar in Penn's Faculty Club. The TV set was on the wall at one end of the bar, and while the others were looking *down* the bar at it, I was underneath it and looking *up* the bar at them. At the far end I could see the only black face there, that of a young bus boy. When the verdict of acquittal was announced every face conveyed dismay. Every face but one.

Half a century after I had left The Hill I wrote a tale about a boy who went there. This story illustrates the way I should have felt at school and college regarding race.

The boy who's at the center of this story wants to integrate his all-white school, and he knows the way to start this is to shake up both the teachers and the other boys. So he decides to bring a black girl to a prom. In a rural black ghetto near the school (and in fact there was one near the Hill School, known to whites as Chicken Hill) he finds the girl he needs. And she, who's even braver than this boy, agrees to be his date.

They fall a little bit in love and once, in fact, have sex. This terribly disturbs her father, a preacher who is much concerned with race.

When the prom takes place, the couple wait outside until, as prearranged, the band starts playing "Stardust." Then they enter, and they dance right down the middle of the hall. Amazed and shocked, the other couples move aside. Though many boys are angry several aren't, and they too dance with the girl. But the couple know they mustn't keep this going too long, and soon they slip outside and leave.

They meet again next day. For whatever cause, her father now has left his family. The boy and girl talk, and she kisses him and walks away. The story ends, "I never saw Estelle again."

This story was the only fiction that I ever wrote, and I've never tried to get it published.

WHILE BLACKS WERE integrating so were Jews, but at a greater speed.

Until the early 1940s Jewish boys did not go to my father's summer camp for boys, Awosting. That's the way it was, but why? I don't believe my father up till then had had a thought-out policy of not admitting Jews. I may be wrong. I'm very sure my mother, a Roosevelt-supporting Democrat, would not have gone along with such a policy if asked. Perhaps he didn't ask and possibly no Jews applied.

No one questioned that Awosting practice till the early 1940s. This was just when Hitler started killing European Jews by millions, though in the U.S.A. this wasn't widely known. As I recall, my father mentioned at the dinner table in the spring of 1942 that a Jewish family had sent him applications for their sons to go to camp. How he knew that they were Jewish I don't know, but he asked my mother what she thought. My older brother Dick chimed in and asked, "Why not?" The upshot was two Jewish boys in camp, and more to come.

When I was a reporter on an Army paper in Trieste one of my colleagues was Jewish, and we got along just fine. However, we had a party for him when he left, and he had too much to drink, and he told me that I was a snob. Apparently he meant that I was anti-Semitic. If I'm an anti-Semite then the pope's a whirling dervish.

In the 1990s I joined a Torah discussion group at Penn. A Jewish engineering professor, Bernard Steinberg, had invited me to be a member. The five of us (I the only gentile) and a rabbi met each week and worked our way through Leviticus and Numbers. Then I asked the other members to read and comment on the draft of a chapter of my book, *The Human Story*, about the history of ancient Israel. Several wrote me helpful comments, but a woman in our little group wrote me an indignant note. It upset her that I had written objectively about such matters as the early history of the *Hapiru*, or Hebrews. She said perhaps I was unknowingly anti-Semitic.

A WASP can hardly live anywhere in America today and not make Jewish friends. Although that's not quite true as yet for blacks and whites, it's on the way.

SEVEN

A Global View

IN MY EARLY 60s I decided that the time had come to leave my job at Penn. I'd had enough of grading papers and exams, and I was blocking the path of some (imagined) younger scholar who could do my job as well as I. Most of all I wanted time to write. I had already started writing something bigger than I'd ever done before.

So I resigned in 1994. My department chairman, Michael Katz, was out of town so he wrote me, saying kindly it was "difficult to assimilate—it is so hard to imagine the department without you."

Our dean, Rosemary Stevens, wrote me a note asking me to lead the faculty procession in the upcoming Arts and Sciences commencement. I wrote and thanked her, and showing off my learning I remarked, "I look forward especially to carrying the mace. Did you know that in the Middle Ages bishops rode their horses into battle armed with maces? They were forbidden to shed blood, but smashing skulls was quite all right."

Commencement

Our children now had flapped their wings and flown away, so we bought a smaller house in Chestnut Hill, a section of Philadelphia that's considered uppercrust. (We are in the filling, not the crust.) The new house isn't far from the old one, and it's one of those "Colonials" that you see below you as your airplane nears its landing and it drones above the suburbs. It isn't far from friends, tennis courts, restaurants where we rarely eat, two local trains that run to Center City, an art museum, a library, and a stream on which my Pennsylvania Dutch great-great-great-(pause)-great-great-great-grandfather Hendrik Sellen ran a mill that squeezed the linseed oil from seeds of flax.

Chestnut Hill has stylish shoppes with names like Hair We Are, Groomingdale's Pet Salon, The Friendly Shop, Spa Elysium Ltd., the Janine Sale de Coiffure, Imperial Accents Inc., the Sunflower Lapel Boutique Inc., Quelque Chose, The Happy Butterfly, The Painted Pansy, Dancing Fairies, and Cuddles N Care, which offers "Quality Day Care in the Private School Manner." My favorite is the Victorian Lady Doll Repair Shop.

Despite the fancy stores, we do have varmints. Deer parade across the lawns, munching the azaleas, telling barking dogs to scram. And we have some lettuce thieves who cause me pangs of guilt:

> I caught a burgling rabbit in a trap,
> The kind of trap that tells you "Have a heart!"
> But doesn't tell you how to gently zap.

From "Victorian" to "Colonial" (by JCD)

I drowned him and I wished I knew that art.
Another time I saw his crooked mate.
Enough of this! I threw a stone and yelled.
No chance I'd hit her but ... my rock flew straight!
It struck her head. She flung her legs and fell.
Our dog though, kills with mind a moral blank;
The killing, not the flesh, is her reward.
She'll gnash the neck and calmly crunch each shank,
Then drop the corpse, with which she now is bored.
    Although I do admire her rite-like mode,
    I hate to kill and don't. "Let live"'s my code.

Another problem here in Chestnut Hill is snow. Once I wrote the *Chestnut Hill Local* asking "Why are those who live in Chestnut Hill's grandest homes the least likely to clear the snow from their sidewalks?" Another reader wrote and gave the answer: "They're sunning in Cancun."

WHILE WE DON'T winter in Cancun we do spend summers in Italy, where Elda owns our modest second home. Her ownership occurred like this. In 1950 Elda's older sister Vida won four million lire in the Italian soccer lottery. Four million lire then were just enough to buy a piece of land and build a bungalow in nearby Sistiana. When Vida died she left this house to Elda, so now we spend our summers there. The house is an easy walk from where Elda's family, whom I wrote about in *Rise from Want*, once lived.

It's also near an ancient rocky road on which I used to jog and now take walks. This road appears on maps that date back to the Middle Ages, but I would bet that shepherds led their baaing beasts along it long before that time, perhaps a thousand years before the Romans took this place. These shepherds' rough corrals of heaped-up rocks survive today on nearby hills.

But I wonder whether people walked this rocky road not just thousands of years but eons before those shepherds led

Sunset and Lightning in Sistiana (by JCD)

their sheep along it. In a cave quite near it archeologists have found the teeth of late *Homo erectus* or early *Homo sapiens.* Hominids camped there, so it seems, as much as half a million years ago. Did they too walk along this path? I sometimes hunt for fossils of those early humans in the rubble of the dig and once I found an ancient molar. I hoped that it was human but an expert said it wasn't.

To give my daily summer walks a goal, I gather seeds from roadside flowers, scratch the dirt in places where they ought by rights to grow, and plant a pinch of seeds and dirt. So far I haven't raised a poppy, but I've fed a lot of ants.

As I walk along the country roads I often picture guiding friends from home and pointing out the things I think they'd like to see: "That's the cave in which they found some early human teeth." "That's the house where "Grasshopper" [a village prostitute] once lived." "Those are trenches dating from the First World War."

A trio of Trieste professor friends—Midio Sussi and Ivo and Aleksander Panjek—and I sometimes go to local farms where one can buy and drink the local wine. The one they call terrano's thick enough to stand on and dark enough to hide in. My friends will never let me pay.

AFTER I RETIRED I carried out the project that I mentioned up above, one that I began while still at Penn.

When *Rise from Want,* my previous book, was published I was 55. For historians, that's young. My mentor at Johns Hopkins, Frederic Lane, was writing (with a former student) a history of Venetian money and banking when he died at the age of 84.[1] To judge by his example I had only started down my road.

Now I wanted to explore a subject broader than the ones I'd written on before. It wasn't that I hoped to make some money, though that would have been a welcome change. What I really wanted was to reach a lot of minds. I didn't want to pour more effort into writing books for academics—casting words before grinds.

I considered writing a history of Europe from the end of the Middle Ages to the French Revolution. That's the age that Penn had hired me to teach about a quarter of a century before. When he listed his course on this subject in Penn's course catalog, the professor who had held my job before me used to call those centuries Europe's "important middle period." Well they are important, but they don't have heaps of sex appeal.

All right, I said, perhaps I ought to write about the Renaissance in Italy. I had often taught a course about that subject, and it *was* an age of mayhem, murder, and Michelangelo. But

as I pondered I had doubts. The Renaissance was brilliant people doing unrelated things. It captivates but doesn't jell.

As I thought about this problem—what to write on—global
history was coming into vogue. Historians now were trying,
as they never had before, to comprehend the whole caboodle,
from early man until today. William McNeill had written a
well-known global history, a book I think is more discussed
than read,[2] and professors who once had taught "western civi-
lization" now were lecturing on the history of the world.

It's true that I had never taught a course on global history.
Others had done it, others do it, others will, but to me the
subject looked impossible to teach. Human beings have simply done too many things to organize in lectures. But could I
write, not teach, about those things? I don't mean could I write
a text, a fact-filled tome for use in courses. No, I had in mind a
book that anyone might like and even learn from.

So I resolved to write a history of the world. That way I
would put to work what skills I had, learn some things I never
knew, and maybe reach a lot of minds. I started on a history
with a vastly bigger sweep than any of the books I'd done before,
one that sketches what mankind has done since early humans
walked along that Carso path I know so well. Pretentiously I
saw myself as like some artist of the Renaissance who switches
from carefully painting tiny miniatures in manuscripts to fres-
coing yards of walls in palaces and churches.

SINCE PEOPLE RARELY read long books today I knew I'd
better make mine short. When I started out, the finest global
history on the market was so big you didn't count the pages.
No, you got some husky friends and weighed it on a scale. The
author, J. M. Roberts, wrote his *History of the World*[3] for an
audience with lots of sitting-flesh. And yet he wrote it well.

I told myself I'd write a book a third as long as his but hopefully as good.

What topics would I deal with in my history of the world? I knew I shouldn't try to "cover" every long-forgotten people. Forget the Mali of Mansa Musa, and the Toltecs of Tulan. As things turned out, I also purposely left out the Assyrians and Turks, the Holy Roman Empire, the Reformation and Enlightenment, not to mention what took place in scores of modern nations.

In the thirty minutes after I decided I would write a global history, chapter titles buzzed inside my brain. I quickly wrote them down, and they totaled 24. In the years that followed, as I wrote the book, I stuck quite closely to that list.

You might suppose that writing something short (compared to Roberts' tome) entails less work, but I don't believe that's true. Writing long is not as hard as writing short.

This is how I worked. For a chapter on a topic that I didn't know a lot about (and there were many) first I read a careful laying-out of facts, possibly an article in the *Encyclopedia Britannica*'s "Macropaedia." Then I read some recent books about the subject, noting where a writer made good points or told a useful anecdote. Next I made an outline and began to write.

I figured that in order not to make the book too long, an average chapter should contain about 8,000 words. That's longer by more than a third than the chapter you are reading now. As I wrote a chapter I would have my computer check the Word Count, and I sometimes found that I was going to finish with, let's say, a thousand words too much. So I constantly revised my outline.

Then I took the chapter I had written to an expert on the subject, usually at Penn, begging him or her to check what I had done. No one ever turned me down. That's a great advantage of being at a university: the access to a sea of expertise. Even some professors I had never met, who had come to Penn after I had left it, helped me out. A Philadelphia high school history teacher, Jerry Ruderman, and my brother Bill, a retired William and Mary English professor to whom this book is dedicated, read the whole ms. and greatly bettered it. Later on an expert copy editor (whose name the publisher will not reveal) made improvements.

Finding the right title for a book can be a problem. For one thing, it's better not to use a name that someone else just used. Years before, as I finished writing *A Venetian Family and Its Fortune,* I thought I'd call it *Family and Fortune,* with a subtitle, but another historian had just used that title,[4] so I had to change the name. I regretted having to do that. After lots of searching for a title for my history of the world, I named it *The Human Story: Our History, from the Stone Age to Today.*

Now that I have told you how I plan and read and note and hunt and peck and count and paste and cut and weep and fuss and fix and check, you can understand just why I write quite slowly. I wrote this global history in my final years at Penn and in the first years after I retired, and the whole job took me 15 years. It's true though that I only did the writing when I had the time to spare—when I wasn't washing dishes; taking walks; hunting forebears on the Web or fossils in a dig; watching "Sixty Minutes"; playing tennis, paying bills, painting walls, cutting grass, or being sawed by surgeons.

I hadn't thought the job would take so long. If I had, perhaps I never would have started.

Only after I had nearly finished writing did I try to find a publisher. I had waited until then because I didn't want to have an editor goading me to hurry up. But now I found an able agent, Richard Balkin, and an editor who liked my manuscript. This editor was Hugh Van Dusen of HarperCollins, the man who had commissioned my *Pursuit of Power* over 30 years before.

HarperCollins published *The Human Story* in hardback in 2004 and then in paperback. As I had planned, it's just about a third as long as Roberts' *History of the World.* You now can buy it in Polish, Spanish, and Japanese translations and it's scheduled to appear in other tongues.

WHEN ANYBODY LEARNED that I was working on a history of the world, he or she was sure to ask me, "What's your thesis? Do you have a point of view?" It's to their credit that they asked; they knew a writer has to have a point of view. But I found their question hard to answer. I sometimes said that since the book has 24 chapters it has two dozen points of view.

However, that's not true. The book does have a general slant, and this is it: In spite of all that many people say, the way we humans live is getting better. On the whole, the news is good. That's also what my previous book, *Rise from Want,* is all about. It shows how one family's lot improved as Europe industrialized.

I used to have a different slant on how the world is doing. In the 1970s I thought, and used to teach my students, that rising population was a monumental problem. I thought it was beyond control, and in 1977 I told a reporter that "The world is in perilous shape. Any thinking person is a little scared by the potential for mass starvation." Today I'm not so scared by growing population as I used to be; our rapid increase may be near its peak.

Most of us forget it, or we never knew it, but until quite recent times the lives of most of those on Earth were hard.

Since then, however, the average living standard has improved a lot.[5] World Bank figures show that in the last half century average real incomes around the world have roughly doubled. Compared to those who went before us, you and I have more to eat and warmer homes. We live a great deal longer and, because of greater literacy and electronic marvels and cheaper travel and more leisure, our lives are richer.

Oh yes, I know that life today continues to be hard for many. Even now, with all of the improvements, roughly half the people in the world still live in makeshift homes and aren't much better off than in the past. And that reminds me: While walking over the South Street Bridge in Philadelphia several years ago I saw a weather-beaten notebook lying near the sidewalk. Someone had penciled on the first page these touching words—and only these: "Ever since I been living as a homeless person I try to think and see if I have learn anything. Most people will say what is there to learn about having nothing. Nothing from nothing leave nothing."

As everybody knows, it isn't only rising wealth that makes things better. For example, medicine today is fast improving and prolonging lives.[6] I am held together fairly well by staples, gold, Dacron tubing, nylon cloth, stainless wire, and something called polymethylmethacrylate. According to a headline that I saw on one of those shock "newspapers" sold at checkout counters, "HEAD TRANSPLANTS NOW POSSIBLE!" But maybe they meant heads of lettuce.

As I neared the end of writing *The Human Story* I wrote a preface that would tell the reader what the book's about. Then I tinkered with it, as I always do, and the sentences became a poem that I put on the final page, as an epilogue. As you'll see, it does reveal a mostly optimistic view.

From Labrador to Coral Sea
Our lives were stunted, bleak, unfree.
We shared our huts with rats and fleas
And lost our children to disease.
(Our holy men would sigh and nod
And tell us "That's the will of God.")

But then, with steam, vaccines, and votes,
Our fortunes rose like tide-raised boats.
We'd more to eat; drew breath more years;
Dethroned (or worse) our tsars, emirs;
Sent men and mirrors as our eyes
To search the black, galactic skies;
And in our cells, till then unseen,
We found our Fates, our djinns: our genes.

The world's still cruel, that's understood,
But once was worse. So far, so good.

However, you object, perhaps our global status isn't good at all; aren't we heating up the world? Most of the experts say we are.[7] Here's one casual observation: During a long drought in the summer of 2003 whole clumps of hornbeam trees in the woods quite near our little house in Italy turned a golden brown, then died. Three years later, in the summer of 2006 the same thing happened once again: We had a solid month of record-breaking heat and drought, and other hornbeams browned and died. So now the leafless, lifeless trunks of trees that died in 2006 stand beside the leafless, lifeless trunks of trees that died three years before. Did global warming done by humans cause those droughts and heat and kill these trees? I wouldn't be surprised.

However, here's another observation that's more cheering. From our house in Italy I can see a little bay, the northernmost tip of the Adriatic Sea, half a mile away. Until perhaps two decades back I rarely saw this inlet's farther shore, but now I see it every day. Apparently this greater visibility results from cleaner air that results from burning cleaner fuels. Beyond the bay I think I see the ancient town of Grado, which traded on the Adriatic well before the rise of Venice. So here's a place where maybe man is doing something right.

Perhaps you also say that this is worse than climate change: The human race (you say) is crueler and more violent than we ever were before. But I'm not sure that's true. Of course I do agree that in the last one hundred years the world has known its share of man-made horrors, including two global wars, Stalin's slaughter, and Hitler's Holocaust.

But is it true that humans weren't so violent in the distant past as in the last one hundred years? As I point out in *The Human Story*, we don't know that and we never will, because our sources of information for ancient history are so few. But we are aware of certain awful deeds that groups of humans did to others long ago. Assyrians not only castrated their captives but impaled them on stakes. Mongol armies slaughtered total populations. In the 1600s Chinese civil wars consumed at least a quarter of that country's people. Later, Arabs, Europeans, and Americans made slaves of many million Africans. These things happened long ago, not yesterday.

When Europeans, centuries back, first arrived in distant regions of the world, they often found the local people making war. For example, when Marco Polo's father and his uncle came to China in the late 1200s they met a ruler who had armies always in the field. Cortés, storming Mexico in the early 1500s, found the Aztecs not only fighting their neighbors but eating them. At about the same time Magellan reached the Philippines, where he found the local people making war. A decade later Pizarro found the Incas in Peru already killing one another even faster than he himself would later do. Those who penetrated Africa in the 1800s often found that deadly wars were under way.

So were we really gentler in the past? I'm sure we used to kill our felons with more zest. An example is the fate of one of my ancestors. Gregory Clement was a London merchant who served on the committee that tried King Charles I of England in 1649, and one of those who signed the warrant for the ruler's death. When Charles's son returned from exile and took power, Clement disguised himself as a servant, but he was spotted (because of his squeaky voice), tried, and put to death.

And here's my point. Clement's sentence was the usual one for traitors. It read in part: "you shall be hanged by the neck and being cut down, your privy members shall be cut off and your bowels taken out and burned before you, your head severed from your body and your body divided into four quarters to be disposed of at the King's pleasure."

IT TOOK ME quite a while to understand that like King Charles I and Gregory Clement I was mortal too. Until I reached my later fifties, I never asked myself how long I'd live. Of course I knew as well as you that death doth take us all. I had written about the historical causes and rates of death in three of my books, and in a course I gave at Penn that I called "Control of Life" I used to lecture on the history of mortality.

As it happens, I'd also been close to other people's deaths. My mother had died of stroke, and my Dad of cigarettes. Once while I was recovering from an operation Elda came to me with upsetting news about a friend. A doctor had suggested that she break it to me slowly, and she did. "Jim," she started, "[Blank] is not too well." "No?" I asked, a bit surprised. "Yes," she said, "in fact, he's very sick." "Are you sure?" I asked, now more concerned. "Yes," she said, "I hate to tell you, but he died last night."

According to a family story some of my ancestors had a baby who died one winter. They held a funeral in their home but, to their horror, when the ceremony started, they could not find the baby in its little coffin! So, no doubt distressed but what else to do?, their cousins and their friends went home. As the last of them picked up his coat from the table in the hall, what do you think he found? You see, I could smile when I heard that family story because I knew quite well that all of us are mortal.

However, I was slow to comprehend that *all* included me. I guess I simply didn't think of that. After all, my mother and most of my aunts and uncles had thrived until they reached about the age of 90. That ripe old age seemed far away.

However, maybe in my later fifties, I had moments of an awful feeling. At times I wondered if I'd ever see another opera live on stage—not that anyone was stopping me from doing that. I had a choking sadness when I thought about my parents; they were gone; I couldn't talk to them. And I simply could not understand these pangs. What on earth was *this* about? I also noticed how the years were racing by; every oldster knows that feeling.

Suddenly it dawned on me: I was understanding at last that I was mortal too.

My mention of those glimpses of my transience brings up something yet more grim. In 1991 I suffered for the first time from depression, and since that year the awful thing has hit me six more times. I'll tell you briefly what depression's like for me. Quite suddenly I'm anxious, sad. But words like sad don't give a sense of what I feel. Everyone I see, including me, is old and weak, and everyone I love is threatened by some danger. Nothing I have done has any worth. And I behave bizarrely. For example, one time while depressed I kept on buying pairs of shoes by mail, two pairs at a time, until I'd purchased ten. All of this goes on for months, sometimes half a year.

One reason why I wrote these memoirs was to cope with bouts of gloom. I wondered: If I rummaged through my mind would I find some dreadful memory I had buried? At the least, I thought, perhaps I'd see myself in full—who I was and what I'd done with my life—and maybe that would help.

I should have looked for help before I did. According to a *Newsweek* poll in 2006, nearly 20 percent of American adults said that they had had some form of therapy, and four percent were currently involved in it.[8] Perhaps those *Newsweek* poll results are true, although the numbers do seem high.

Eventually I did consult a psychoanalyst, and we talked through many aspects of my life. He urged me repeatedly to search inside myself and talk about the things I'd rather leave unsaid. He used to push me into voicing what was lurking in my mind. We concluded I had not squelched some dreadful memory. What I learned about myself in therapy didn't turn on lights, revealing buried horrors. Instead of that a general awareness of who I am seeped inside my mind.

I always do recover. After maybe half a year, the gloom lets up, the sun is shining once again. Today, it looks just possible that the combination of talk therapy and more effective medicine will help me to avoid depression in the future. I'm not counting on it.

What's strange is this: Although I'm subject to depression—and that's a big "although"—I've been lucky all my life. Lucky in my parents, lucky in my schooling, lucky in being sent to

Italy (and not to war), lucky in meeting Elda, lucky in landing a job I liked, and lucky in our children. My psychiatrist has
suggested that all of those good things weren't luck. He suggests I made them happen, and I'd like to think he's right.

WELL, WHAT ARE aging and retirement like? Do I miss
teaching, which I did for a third of a century? No, I don't. The
only thing better than teaching is not teaching.

I'm busy. You should see my long, computerized To Do list.
As fast as I can I DO one thing and DELETE it from the list, I
INSERT another.

I follow politics a bit. As a young man (i.e., in my late 40s
and early 50s) I even served for a while as a Democratic "com-
mitteeman." (That's the lowest level in Philadelphia politics,
un-paid, un-thanked.) But when it comes to politics today I
mainly read the news and grouse.

A year before the election of 2008 I wrote some breezy lines
about "The Candidates" and put them in our Season's Greetings letter. Here are five of those contenders, accompanied by
(on the next page) an illustration I drew by computer:

> The joint will jump if we choose Hil.
> (First Gent will be the randy Bill.)
> The gov with mile-long résumé
> Is Richardson, from Santa Fe.
> Obama warned, "Avoid Iraq!"
> McCain says, "Beat 'em blue and black!"
> Remember Edwards—ran for Veep?
> (Instead we got the surly creep.)
> With things as bad as each one says,
> How come they want to serve as Prez?

By the time you read this, most of the candidates will be
forgotten.

W. Clinton in pursuit, Richardson with c.v., McCain (by JCD)

Here's a thing I never had the time to do before retirement:

I joined an oldsters' luncheon group.
We dine each month on snapper soup.
We gossip, reminisce, and kvetch,
And criticize the White House wretch.

I still have lunch with them each month and a friend and I have organized another monthly luncheon group. Today such groups are widely known as ROMEOs, meaning Retired Old Men Eating Out. Women ought to have such groups and call them DOLLs, meaning Dear Old Ladies Lunching.

Once a week I eat at Penn with other retirees, men I've known for decades. Once this group was called "the English table" but now the only English scholar in our group is Robert Turner, whose students used to call him "the divine Turner." His specialty was Shakespeare but today, he says, he does a thousand other things but never reads the Bard.

What else? I do some painting but I'm over-cautious; I need to dare, to run some risks. In a movie once I heard about a second-grade teacher whose pupils painted boldly, like Matisse. This teacher told her friends her secret was to snatch away their paintings at the proper time.

You could do this too, so you ought to be informed. Elda and I have twice had backyard "Pollock Painting Parties." Painting

Pollock painters (Elda and I at left)

in the Jackson Pollock manner, three generations of our family dripped and dribbled the residue in cans of latex paint on trash-picked hunks of plywood. Our son Daniel even dipped his hands in paint and *hurled* it. The results were great, and in 2007 we had a show of 13 peoples' paintings (two apiece) at the University of Pennsylvania.

Each day at five p.m. I drink a 3/3/3 martini "on the rocks": 3 oz., 3 of gin to 1 vermouth, and 3 cubes of ice. Why three ounces? Medical researchers say that male heart patients should have two drinks a day, and I read somewhere that two drinks equal three ounces. Women, so they say, should have a single drink a day, not two. I love what happens as you pour the strong stuff on the ice: the way it cracks and snaps.

I'VE TYPED SOME NOTES called "Information Regarding James and Elda Davis," and I keep them on my desk. Our children will find them useful if Elda and I die at the same time.

Among a lot of other things, this "Information" mentions this: "For burial plots, see the file [in my desk] labeled

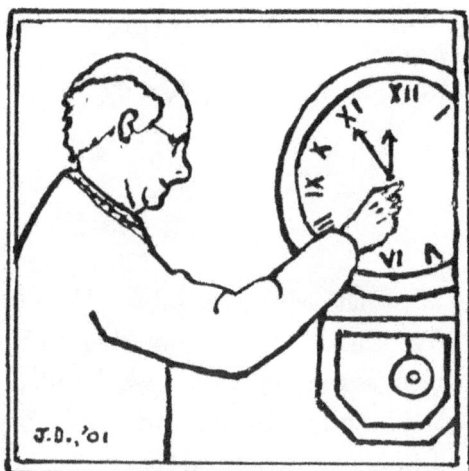

Eleventh hour (by JCD)

BURIAL, which contains old deeds for two plots in [...] Cemetery, Phoenixville, PA. The cemetery people say (see their letter in the file) that the spaces still exist."

About those plots: Soon after the Civil War my great-grandfather, John Griffen (the cannon maker), purchased a piece of land in that cemetery big enough for 16 graves. Four of my great-grandparents, two of my grandparents, and about eight other relatives are buried there, and Elda and I have the deeds for the last two places. I sometimes fantasize about being there with the old ones and chatting with them, the way the dead folks do in a graveyard at the end of Thornton Wilder's play, *Our Town.* However, I suspect that some of my ancestors used more space for their graves than they should have, and it may turn out there isn't room for us.

Well *we* won't care.

What Next?

It's what we've always done: We innovate.
We learned to stand, and then to hack with stones,
And as the ages passed we founded states
And mastered steam and probed beyond the known.
But have you noticed that we've raised our pace?
That now we throw what's out of date away
And revolutionize the human race
Not now and then but, so it seems, each day?
We're told the news: "You've heard?" "No, what about?"
"They've cloned a sheep!" (Or maybe "Smallpox checked!"
Or "North Pole melts!" Or "God and Marx in doubt!")
And, shocked the umpteenth time, we cry, "What next?"
    You know that Chinese curse, "I wish that you
    Will live in interesting times"? We do.

NOTES

Chapter 1: Joiner of Circles

1. Theresa and Frank Caplan, *The Early Childhood Years: The 2- to 6-Year-Old* (1983), 4–5, 33, 106, 204, 236, 268; Nicky Hayes, *Psychology* (2003), 28–29.

2. Claudia Clark, *Radium Girls: Women and Industrial Health Reform, 1910–1935* (1997).

3. "Growing Up in an Iron Town at the Turn of the Century: A Memoir by John Griffen Pennypacker," *Pennsylvania History*, LXIV (1977), 233–48.

4. For a contrast with my pallid boyhood experience of the war, see Robert MacNeil's account of his doings in *Wordstruck: A Memoir* (1989), chapters 2 and 3; and Peter Gay's *My German Question: Growing Up in Nazi Berlin* (1998).

Chapter 2: Hunter of Truth

1. Mills wrote the words and Ellington the tune.

2. I particularly liked the writing of a *New York Times* reporter, Meyer Berger. See his *The Eight Million: Journal of a New York Correspondent* (1983).

Chapter 3: Cold Warrior

1. Walter LaFeber, *America, Russia, and the Cold War, 1945–2002* (9th ed., 2002), is an overview of big events mentioned in this chapter.

2. David H. Hackworth, *Hazardous Duty* (1996), 10.

3. *A Bowl of Cherries: The Memoirs of Tom Boyd from 1932 to 1992* (1992), 70.

4. Boyd, *Bowl*, 71.

5. It meant a lot to all of us. See my article, "Zone A in the Early 1950s, as We Americans Knew It," *Acta Histrae,* 14 (2006, 1), 141–54.

Chapter 4: On My Way

1. A few examples by well-known people are Russell Baker, *Growing Up* (1982) and *The Good Times* (1989); Moss Hart, *Act One* (1959); MacNeil, *Wordstruck* (1989); Willie Morris, *North toward Home* (1967); and Artur Rubinstein, *My Young Years* (1973).

2. Alan Charles Kors, *Atheism in France, 1650–1729* (1990); Richard S. Dunn, *Sugar and Slavery: The Rise of the Planter Class in the English West Indies, 1624–1713* (1972); Thomas C. Childers, *The Nazi Voter: The Social Foundations of Fascism in Germany, 1919–1933* (1983); F. Hilary Conroy, publications on Japan; Marc Trachtenberg, *Constructed Peace: The Making of the European Settlement, 1945–1963* (1999).

3. *Pursuit of Power: Venetian Ambassadors' Reports on Turkey, Spain, and France in the Age of Philip II, 1560–1600* (1970).

Chapter 5: Lives of Rich and Poor

1. Davis, *Venetian Family.*

2. Howard Corning, ed., "A Letter from John Griffen, Ironmaster, 1878: A Description of Improvements in the Manufacture of Iron, Pennsylvania, 1843–1878," *Journal of Economic and Business History*, III (1931), 687–703.

3. "A Slovene Laborer and His Experience of Industrialization, 1888–1976," *East European Quarterly*, 10 (1976), 3–19.

4. Editrice Goriziana (1988).

5. University of Pennsylvania Press (1986).

Chapter 6: Wordstruck Klutz

1. Howard Gardner, *Intelligence Re-framed: Multiple Intelligences for the 21st Century* (1999), esp. 27–46.

2. Hayes, *Psychology*, 83–84.

3. *In Search of History* (1978).

4. *Doing Battle: The Making of a Skeptic* (1995), 249, 253.

5. For the big picture see Martin Campbell-Kelly and William Aspray, *Computer: A History of the Information Machine* (2004).

Chapter 7: A Global View

1. Lane and Reinhold C. Mueller, *Money and Banking in Medieval and Renaissance Venice* (1985).

2. *The Rise of the West: A History of the Human Community* (1963).

3. Revised, 1993.

4. Lawrence Stone, *Family and Fortune: Studies in Aristocratic Finance in the Sixteenth and Seventeenth Centuries* (1973).

5. Joseph E. Stiglitz, *Roaring Nineties: A New History of the World's Most Prosperous Decade* (2003), is a readable overview.

6. Ray Porter, *The Greatest Benefit of Mankind: A Medical History of Humanity* (1997).

7. On climate change see Gale E. Christianson, *Greenhouse: The 200-Year Story of Global Warming* (1999); and J. R. McNeil, *Something New Under the Sun: An Environmental History of the Twentieth-Century World* (2000).

8. March 27, 2006, p. 45.

INDEX

A

Adriatic Sea, 129–30
advantages, growing up with, ix
African-Americans. See blacks
    (African-Americans)
age
    gap in, between parent and child,
        2–3
    and historians, 123
air, quality of, 129–30
ambassadors, Venetian, 77–78
American Historical Review, The, 76
Americanization, of immigrants, 89
antiquity, fascination with, 15–16
anti-Semitism. *See* Jews and
        anti-Semitism
Army. *See* U.S. Army
Austria-Hungary, 41, 49, 125
awareness of time and place
    J. C. Davis's expanding, 1–18
    typical development in children, 1
Awosting, Camp, 2, 7, 11–16, 117

B

baby book, 1–2
Bacon, Francis, 33
Baker, James A., III, 24
baseball, 13–14
basic training, 37
Becker, James P., 37–38, 44, 48, 60
blacks (African-Americans), 28, 35,
        73, 89–90, 113–18, 130

blah, mindless, 105–106
bloopers, 73
Blue Devil, The, 44–45, 117–18
Bologna, 47, 68
    University of, 69
books and articles by J. C. Davis, 10,
        28, 32–34, 36, 60–61, 76–77, 81,
        84, 93–99, 121, 124–27
Boyd, Tom, 40, 44, 48, 60
Braudel, Fernand, 76, 83
Bronx, N.Y., 87, 89
Brown, Judith, 71
burial plots, 136–37

C

camp, family experiences at, 2, 7,
        11–16, 117
Carnegie, Andrew, 93
Carso, the, 43, 49, 50
Caruso, Enrico, 5
chairmanship, of History Depart-
        ment, 74
change, global and human, 129–
        31, 138
chaperones, at Princeton, 31–32
character, emphasis on, at Camp
        Awosting, 12
Chestnut Hill Local, The, 121
children
    of J. C. Davis, 107–10
    of Venetian nobles, 81–83
"circles" of awareness, 1–18

class, social, 7–8, 21, 25–26, 91. *See also* Venice: ruling class
clothing
  at The Hill School, 20
  in postwar Trieste, 42
  at Princeton, 25–26
clubs, Princeton, 25–26
Cold War, 37, 42–43, 45, 47–48
Columbia University, 58, 65
committee work, at University of Pennsylvania, 78–79
"Control of Life," course on, 71
courses, Princeton, 65–66, 69
cultural anthropology, 30

D

Daily Princetonian, The, 26, 27, 28, 33, 35, 114
Davis, Daniel R., 61, 93, 107–10
Davis, David J., 59, 93, 107–10
Davis, Elda Z., ix, 48–55, 61–62, 97, 107–10, 121, 131–32
Davis, Mary P. *See* parents, of J. C. Davis
Davis, Miriam. *See* Lally, Miriam D.
Davis, Richard P., 1, 3, 13
Davis, William F., Junior, v, 1, 3, 126
Davis, William Faber (senior). *See* parents, of J. C. Davis
Decline of the Venetian Nobility as a Ruling Class, The, 76, 84
Depression, Great, 4, 6–7
depression, psychological, 99, 132–33
diet, 62, 92, 95–96, 107, 129
discipline, of students, 8, 20
discrimination. *See* blacks (African-Americans); Jews and anti-Semitism; women, roles of
dissertation, doctoral
  by J. C. Davis, 61, 62–63
  supervised by J. C. Davis, 73

DOLL (Dear Old Ladies Lunching), 135
Donà dalle Rose family, 80–84, 102
dowries, 82–83
drawings by J. C. Davis. *See* paintings and drawings by J. C. Davis
dreams, meaning of, 101–3
Duino Castle
  dues to lord of, 94–95
  located on map, 39

E

Episcopalians, Davis ancestors as, 91–92
examination, J. C. Davis's final, at Johns Hopkins, 64
executions, for treason, 131

F

fantasies, by J. C. Davis, 14, 35–36
fellowships, difficulty in obtaining, 56, 58
fertility, in Donà family, 111
fiction, by J. C. Davis, 116–17
fighting, at The Hill School, 22
Fulbright scholarships, 61, 68

G

genetics, understanding of, 129
girls, experiences with, 19, 22, 30–32, 35, 39, 42, 72
global history, as a subject, 124
God, reflections about, 23, 28, 30, 40, 129, 138
grades
  earned at Princeton, 27, 28, 57, 70
  incident with student, 72
graduate school and teaching, 56–59, 73–74
grandchildren, party given by, 110
Gritti, Andrea, 60–63, 70

H

Hall, Walter P., 25
Hans Brinker or the Silver Skates,
 6, 17
HarperCollins, 78, 127
Harvard University, 65
"Heartland," U.S. *See* Middle West
Hill School, The, 19–24, 113
history, as a subject of study, ix,
 55–56, 72–73, 75
 experiences of J. C. Davis with,
  15–16, 47, 55–56, 57–58, 60, 62,
  123–31
Hitler, Adolf, 72–73, 130
Homo sapiens, early years of, 122,
 138
houses, of Davis and Žužek families
 and ancestors, 87, 92–94, 120–21
*Human Story, The: Our History, from
 the Stone Age to Today,* 124–27

I

iambs, 104
immigration, 43, 67, 86–87
income
 of Davis ancestors, 92–93
 trends in world, 128
India, 111–12
Indians, American, 13, 15–16, 86,
 87, 90
industry and the Industrial Revolution, 5, 91, 96–97, 127
intelligence, nature of, 99
Internet, research via, 85
iron-making, 1, 15, 91, 93
Istanbul, 40–41, 60
Italian-Americans, 5, 43

J

Jews and anti-Semitism, 21, 31,
 117–18

Johns Hopkins University, 58–61,
 64, 114–15
jury service, 115–16

K

Kipling, Rudyard, 10
klutz, experiences as a, 99–102
Korean War, 34, 38

L

Lally, John C., 68
Lally, Miriam D., 66, 93, 107–10
Lane, Frederic, 58–60, 123
language(s)
 at The Hill School, 20–21
 learning new, 45–46
 of the Slovene people on the
  Carso, 50, 52–53
 and spelling reform, 107
 translating, 77
limericks, 105–106, 110
living standards, 50–51, 128–29
luck, sense of, 133–34

M

Macintosh, Mia, ix, 105
MacNeil, Robert, 103
marriage
 Davis-Žužek, 51–54
 among Venetian nobles, 63,
  82–83
martini cocktails, 136
Marx, Karl, 80
Mayflower, 86
McNeill, William, 124
medicine, advances in, 128, 133, 138
memoirs, by other writers, 10, 19,
 40, 103, 140
 typical ending of, 66
Middle West, 23, 64
mortality, 63, 88–89, 94–96, 131–32

N

naked women
   and ancestral archbishop, 86
   early glimpses of, 17, 27
names
   appreciation of, 106
   of contemporaries, 12, 36, 43, 89
   of Davis family forebears, 1, 89
Native Americans. *See* Indians,
   American
neatness and orderliness, 13, 101
Newark Star-Ledger, The, 34–35
New York City, 6, 23–24
New York Times, The, 35, 68
"nice," as a student evaluation, 71
nobility. *See* Venice: ruling class

O

Oberdorfer, Don, 27
Oberlin College, 23–24, 64–65
opportunities, prize for "taking
   advantage of," 13
Orange, N.J., 5–6, 34
orientation, Army, 42–43
others, awareness of existence of,
   1, 56

P

painting (and other arts), 27, 47, 84,
   104, 135–36
paintings and drawings by J. C.
   Davis, 67, 120, 122, 135, 137
parents, of J. C. Davis, 1–4, 6–7, 19,
   20–21, 23, 132
Pennsylvania, University of, 65–66,
   113, 116, 119
Pennsylvania State University, 58
Personnel Committee, University of
   Pennsylvania, 78–79
perspective, as reason for studying
   history, 73

Ph.D., J. C. Davis's work on, 58, 61,
   64, 65, 66
Philadelphia, 66–67, 71, 103
Philadelphia Inquirer, The, 68
Pirenne, Henri, 27
poems by J. C. Davis, 105, 129, 134
politics, participation in, 134
Pompeii, 40–41
population growth, 127
poverty, 6, 42, 71, 80, 111, 127. *See
   also* class, social
prayer, 9–10
prep school. *See* Hill School, The
presidents, U.S., 59, 64
Princeton Alumni Weekly, The, 31–32,
   113
Princetonian, The Daily, 26, 27, 28,
   33, 35, 114
Princeton University, 2, 23–26, 29,
   36, 113
prostitution, 17, 41, 58, 82, 122–23
psychoanalysis, 100, 102, 133–34
psychology, 27, 101
Pursuit of Power, 77

Q

Quakers, 85, 91

R

racism and race relations. *See* blacks
   (African-Americans)
radium, 5, 18
Reformation, Protestant, 85, 125
"relevance," of university courses,
   70–71
religion, 8–11, 23, 28–30, 40, 47,
   91, 129
Renaissance, Italian, 71, 123–24
reporting
   for *The Blue Devil,* 44–45
   for *The Newark Star-Ledger,* 34–35

for school and college papers, 27–28, 32–33

research, academic, role of, 65, 74–75

reviews, of books by J. C. Davis, 76, 83, 97

Rise from Want, 93–99, 121, 127

Roberts, J. M., 124, 127

Robeson, Paul, 28, 114

rocks, interest in, 13, 14

ROMEO (Retired Old Men Eating Out), 135

Russell, Bertrand, 29

S

scholarships and fellowships, 23, 58, 61, 64, 66, 68

schooling
    prep school. *See* Hill School, The
    public elementary school, 7–8
    university. See Johns Hopkins University; Pennsylvania State University; Princeton University

self-knowledge, 1, 99

servants, of Davis ancestors, 92–93

sex
    attempt of colonists to control, 88
    youthful discoveries about, 16–17, 22

Sistiana, Italy, 121–23

slavery, 89–90, 130

Slovene (language), 44, 50, 52

snobbery, 25–26. *See also* class, social

solipsism, 1, 56

"sorry to inform you," 57, 66

sources, historical, 60, 63, 77, 93–98

spearheads, 15–16

spelling reform, 107

spoiling, alleged, by mother, 2

sports, involvement in, 13–14
    boxing match, 22
    See also tennis

Stace, Willard, 28–29

Studi veneziani, 61

"Sundance Kid," 15

Svevo, Italo, 100–101

T

teaching, 3, 25, 57, 59, 69, 71, 74, 79, 102, 134

tennis, 13, 32, 102, 126

tenure, 77–79

"Tisket, a Tasket, A," 7

Toronto, University of, 65

travel, as means of broadening world view
    in India, 111–12
    in Italy, 46–47

trees, dying from drought, 129

Trieste, 38–39, 41–42, 100
    map of area around, 39
    riots in, 47–48

"truth," search for, 19, 22–23, 28–30

Turkey, 60–61, 63, 125

Turner, Frederick Jackson, 59

U

universities
    advantages of, 75, 125–26
    growth of American, 57

U.S. Army, 37, 54, 113–14

V

Venetian Family and Its Fortune, A, 81

Venice, 46–47, 60
    ruling class, 62–63, 76

Victorian Lady Doll Repair Shop, 120

Vietnam War, 67–68

violence, in human history, 130–31
Vižovlje, Italy, 49–51, 95, 97

W

war, in human history, 130–31
WASPs, WASCs, and WMASPs,
  85, 113–14
wealth, 5, 70, 80, 82, 91–92,
  111–12
wedding, Davis-Žužek, 54
White, Theodore, 103
William and Mary, College of, 126
Wolff, Tobias, 19

women, roles of, 112–13
word-processing, appreciation for,
  105
"wordstruck," 73, 99, 105–106
world history, as a subject, 124
World War I, 2, 17, 41, 97, 123
World War II, 17–19, 50, 97
writing
  learning, 32–34
  process of, 103–104, 125–26

Z

Žužek family, 48–55, 93–97, 121

www.ingramcontent.com/pod-product-compliance
Lightning Source LLC
Chambersburg PA
CBHW032133040426
42449CB00005B/222